BIRMINGHAM CITY TRANSPORT

TRANSPORT

FROM TRAMS TO BUSES IN THE CORONATION YEAR

WORTHING BUS RALLY
28 July 2013.

Front cover images:

2691

The bus working on the Inner Circle 8 route in Farm Street, Hockley, has just passed the Joseph Lucas & Son factory. This factory was originally built as the Electric Lighting & Dynamo factory and during the period of the Coronation the Farm Street frontage was extensively decorated. The inner suburbs of the city were still largely made up of nineteenth-century houses and were occupied mainly by factory workers, many of whom had fought in both world wars. This led to the patriotic feelings which led to street parties and, as with the terraced houses on the left, to flags and bunting decorating the houses. The bus is 2691 (JOJ 691), a Metro-Cammell-bodied Daimler CVD6 which at the time was allocated to the nearby Hockley garage. (D. R. Harvey Collection)

616

Despite the appalling and crudely written 'BIRMINGHAMS LAST TRAM', even painted without an apostrophe, right up to the end there was a feeling that the trams had to look smart. On the morning of 4 July 1953, in Miller Street depot, one of the lady cleaners washes down the Brush Burnley bogies of Brush-bodied car 616, as her reflection positively shines on the rocker panel of the tram. (D. R. Harvey Collection)

BIRMINGHAM CITY TRANSPORT

TRANSPORT

FROM TRAMS TO BUSES IN THE CORONATION YEAR

DAVID HARVEY

AMBERLEY

Acknowledgements

My sincere thanks are accorded to Alan Wycherley for allowing me to use the photographs of the late Norman Glover and Les Perkins and to David Packer for allowing me to use the photographs of Gerry Dunglas. Many of the remaining photographs were acquired from the original photographers and most of these died many years ago, remembering that nearly all these photographs are sixty years old. Elsewhere, the photographs which are not credited on the print and therefore the photographer cannot be traced are credited to my own extensive collection, which I have built up over the last forty years. I would also like to thank my wife Diana for proof reading skills and suggestions for this book

First published 2013

Amberley Publishing
The Hill, Stroud
Gloucestershire, GL5 4EP

www.amberley-books.com

Copyright © David Harvey 2013

The right of David Harvey to be identified as the Author
of this work has been asserted in accordance with the
Copyrights, Designs and Patents Act 1988.

All rights reserved. No part of this book may be reprinted
or reproduced or utilised in any form or by any electronic,
mechanical or other means, now known or hereafter invented,
including photocopying and recording, or in any information
storage or retrieval system, without the permission in writing
from the Publishers.

British Library Cataloguing in Publication Data.
A catalogue record for this book is available from the British Library.

ISBN 978 1 4456 1496 0
E-Book ISBN: 978-1-4456-1499-1

Typeset in 10pt on 12pt Sabon.
Typesetting and Origination by Amberley Publishing.
Printed in the UK.

Contents

Victoria Square

The view across Victoria Square towards the Council House in June 1953 shows flags, banners and bunting hanging from every available point. Even the statue of Queen Victoria is subsumed by decorative flags. In front of the Council House are a couple of 'New Look front' buses while in the foreground is a Fordson E83 van. (The late Dr P. Nicklin)

Introduction

The aim of this book is to try to capture, through the city municipal transport system, how Birmingham looked in 1953. Socially and economically, Birmingham was a very different place to the thriving Second City of the United Kingdom in the Twenty-First Century. Birmingham was barely getting over the trauma of the Second World War and the infamous reconstructions of the 1960s were still on the drawing board, yet change was in the air. The Coronation of Queen Elizabeth II and the associated celebrations and the final closure of the last tram routes meant that it was the year which saw the 'out with the old' and, with the dawn of what Winston Churchill referred to as 'The New Elizabethan' age, 'in with the new'.

The book is therefore divided into two halves; firstly there are the changes in the bus fleet, which had grown by 1953 into a fleet size of around 1,700 vehicles, while secondly there are the Coronation celebrations exemplified by decorations both on the buses and in the streets through which they operated from the City Centre to the suburbs. Finally, there is the changeover from the departing trams to the new replacement bus services. The second part of the book looks at the final three existing tramcar routes and shows the events of the last day on Saturday 4 July, the final transfer of trams away from the last operating depot at Miller Street and the eventual breaking up of the tram fleet over the next month.

1761

During the celebrations for the Coronation, even out in the suburbs, smaller shops suddenly began to display their patriotism. Coventry Road, Small Heath, was no exception, with the well-known bakery and confectionery shops owned by A. D. Wimbush being decorated with Union Jack bunting while the shops behind the bus all have Union Jack flags flying. On Friday 5 June 1953, in much better weather than for the Coronation three days earlier, a well-laden Daimler CVD6, 1761 (HOV 761), equipped with Coronation flags, travels past the junction with St Oswald's Road as it goes on its way to Wagon Lane, Sheldon, on the 58C shortworking. This had been introduced as a trolleybus turn back on 24 January 1949. These Daimler-engined Daimlers were very quiet and sophisticated and it was always suggested that they were sent to Coventry Road garage after the trolleybus abandonment on 30 June 1951 because they were the nearest thing to the 'Silent Service'. (Omnibus Society)

Buses Celebrating the Coronation

Princess Elizabeth ascended the throne as Queen of the United Kingdom, Canada, Australia, New Zealand, South Africa, Ceylon, and Pakistan, as well becoming the Head of the Commonwealth on the death of her father, the late King George VI, on 6 February 1952. She was proclaimed Queen Elizabeth II by her various privy and executive councils shortly afterwards. The Coronation, after sixteen months of preparation and at a cost of £2 million, was held on 2 June 1953. 7,500 guests were squeezed into Westminster Abbey, while for the first time the Coronation was shown by the BBC on their still-new television service, which attracted an estimated audience of 20.4 million viewers, while radio had another 11.7 million listeners.

In most parts of the country, town and city centres vied with each other to produce the most spectacular street decorations, which were largely sponsored by the local authority, but in the larger urban centres, the bigger shops, office blocks and factories produced equally spectacular feasts of patriotic red, white and blue bunting and Union Flags. Streets were deserted on the morning of Coronation Day, Tuesday 2 June 1953, but came to life as soon as the Coronation ceremony in London had finished. This led to the start of thousands of street parties up and down the land, with residential streets converted into a sort of open-air canteen where children and adults alike feasted on sandwiches, pork pies, cakes and blancmange and jelly. Every school child had received a celebratory Coronation mug and these, as well as Union Jack hats, paper napkins, red, white and blue paper table cloths and balloons and bunting, adorned most streets.

As the Second City, Birmingham's central decorations were an extravagant and dazzling riot of colour which brightened up the then somewhat dowdy city centre, while it should be remembered that throughout the city the scars of the wartime bombing were still there, with huge, gaping spaces which had once been thriving department stores and shops. The Coronation was really the first opportunity for the ordinary person in the street to let their hair down and actually celebrate something after six long years of war and an even longer period of austerity and rationing.

Corporation-Operated Transport in the City

The transport operated by the local Birmingham City Transport department by 1953 consisted of three linked tram routes and 104 tramcars which were due for final closure on 4 July 1953. The Transport Committee decided that there would be no decorated tramcar as there had been in 1911, 1937 and 1945 on the grounds that the old, outdated trams would not be missed. The bus fleet was nearly all post-war buses by this time, with all the wartime buses gone, the Coventry Road trolleybuses prematurely withdrawn two years earlier and barely one hundred pre-war buses still operating. The policy of wiping away everything and replacing it with a new bus fleet would have repercussions early in the next decade when new vehicles would be required in quite large numbers, but that was something to worry about later. For the Coronation, it was decided that every bus would be fitted with a pair of Coronation flags and these were to be located at the front of the bus beneath the destination box. Each bus was fitted with a small bracket with two holes and on to these were affixed the flags. It was tasteful and conservative and was a feature which matched the distinguished blue and cream livery of the bus fleet. This was in complete contrast to the shabbily presented tram 616, the final tramcar, which brought up the rear of the final procession to Erdington ran just over one month after the Coronation.

Buses Celebrating the Coronation

Buses Wearing Flags

As part of the city-wide Coronation celebrations, as well as the usual proclaiming street-wide banners, Union flags and bunting, the City Transport Department placed two small brackets below the front destination box of all the post-war buses numbered from 1481 to 2998 and 3000. The first of the MOF-registered Guy Arab IVs, 3006, 3008, 3010–11, 3013–16 and 3018 to 3020, were also delivered in time to have the flag holders fitted. A very few of the surviving pre-war fleet of Daimler COG5s were also fitted with flag brackets.

2489
Preserved Birmingham City Transport Crossley bus 2489 (JOJ 489) shows the Coronation Union flags located in the bracket mounted on the guttering below the front destination box. The bracket had two small holes drilled into it and it was through these that the two small flags were fitted. (D. R. Harvey)

For the benefit of those interested in the Birmingham bus fleet, the vehicles are shown in numerical order.

1488

Travelling along Witton Lane in June 1953 is 1488 (GOE 488), a Daimler CVA6 with a Metro-Cammell H30/24R which had entered service on 17 July 1947 and was only the eighth post-war bus. The bus is approaching the Witton Square terminus of the 39 bus route and has just passed Villa Park, home of Aston Villa. Just visible is the pair of Coronation flags mounted on the brackets just below the centre of the destination box. On the left is Witton tram depot, which was built in 1882 to house the steam trams of the Birmingham & Aston Tramways Company, who operated a public service between the Old Square and Witton. The main shed still survives, with its inscription 'BOROUGH OF ASTON MANOR TRAMWAYS DEPOT' just visible over the central pair of the four arched entrances, and for many years was the home of the late lamented Aston Manor Transport Museum. Closed as a running shed on 30 September 1950, in November 1952 the depot was reopened for night storage and some docking work. The tram on the extreme left is car 656, one of the MRCW totally-enclosed 63-seaters with English Electric 40hp motors and mounted on EMB Burnley maximum traction bogies. (Birmingham Central Reference Library)

1558

Loading up at a temporary bus stop outside the Three Horseshoes public house in June 1953, is 1558 (GOE 558). It is operating on the 45C shortworking route through Stirchley towards the city centre, with Umberslade Road and the TASCO Co-Operative in the background. The overloaded Metro-Cammell-bodied Daimler CVG6 was transferred to Cotteridge garage after the 1952 abandonment of the Pershore Road 36 tram service. Wearing the crossed Coronation flags, 1558 entered service on 1 November 1947 and so was already well over five years old. These CVG6s were some of the most iconic-looking early post-war exposed radiator BCT buses with their snout-like bonnet concealing the lengthy Gardner 6LW 8.4 litre engine. Virtually identical buses were supplied to Edinburgh and Newcastle Corporations when those municipalities opted for MCCW, BCT-style bodies in order to get a quicker delivery date. (S. N. J. White)

1739

On Thursday 11 June 1953, 1739 (HOV 739) passes the flag-bedecked Birchfield Cinema in Birchfield Road, Perry Barr. This is another one of the 100-strong batch of Leyland Titan PD2/1s with Brush coachwork which were delivered between March 1948 and May 1949. The buses were divided between Yardley Wood and Perry Barr garages, with the last fifty-seven allocated to the latter garage. 1739 is travelling into the city on the 33 service from Kingstanding and is carrying an advertisement for Walker Brother's electrical shop, who sold the then very popular Ecko radios and televisions which had been sold in large numbers in order to listen to or watch the Queen's Coronation just ten days earlier. New advertising contracts had only been contracted with potential customers in the spring of 1953 in order to place advertisements on the bus fleet as once the closure of the tram system occurred on 4 July a replacement source of revenue would have to be found. Up until this time buses had rarely carried advertisements save for wartime missives to save or buy war bonds and it was only in about April 1953 that buses began to carry advertisements. (D. R. Harvey Collection)

1733 (Opposite, below)

When the author was a very little boy, 1733 (HOV 733), a Leyland Titan PD2/1 with a Brush H30/24R body, was his favourite Birmingham bus. These one hundred buses were designated PD2 Specials by Leyland Motors. The bus is carrying an early advertisement for Kellogg's Corn Flakes. At the end of May 1953, 1733 stands in Bull Street outside the decorated Grey's department store. GOD SAVE THE QUEEN, the E II R monogram and the red, white and blue flagging and bunting almost hide the front of this, one of the city's most prestigious shops. Grey's had opened in 1891 and advertised itself for many years as 'Birmingham's Own Store'. It was taken over by the Debenhams Group at the end of February 1973. 1733 is standing almost on the spot where a bomb exploded in October 1940, causing the death of several people and leaving behind a huge crater. (F. W. York)

1770

This line-up of buses in Perry Barr garage yard in June 1953 shows conclusively that pre-war buses did carry Coronation flags! On the left is MCCW-bodied Daimler CVD6 1770 (HOV 770), while next to it, with one of the garage fitters standing in front of the registration plate, is an unidentified 1937-vintage, CVP-registered Daimler COG5. Affixed to the front are a pair of Union Jack flags while at the far end of the line is 1179 (FOF 179), another pre-war COG5 but this time built in 1939. This bus is also adorned with a pair of miniature flags, which were not usually fitted to the pre-war bus fleet. Between the two pre-war buses is 2349 (JOJ 349), an exposed-radiator Crossley DD42/6 with a Crossley body, and 1740 (HOV 740), one of the large batch of Brush-bodied Leyland Titan PD2/1s which would spend over nineteen years until June 1968 working on the arduous services operated from Perry Barr. (L. Deakin)

2178

Unloading its passengers at the top of Livery Street is flag-bedecked 2178 (JOJ 178). This Leyland-bodied Leyland Titan PD2/1 has come into the city centre on a 72 service, which went as far as the Birmingham-West Bromwich boundary at the Woodman public house, although the stop was more famous for being about one hundred yards from the West Bromwich Albion turnstiles at the Hawthorns. All the Soho Road services terminated in Livery Street and, once unloaded, turned the corner into Colmore Row. The buses would then turn left where the railings are behind the pedestrians before pulling up outside the main entrance of Snow Hill Station on a short section of road which faced against the rest of the normal traffic and formed a buses-only road. There were fifty of these non-standard buses in the BCT fleet; they were very fleet of foot and spent their entire lives allocated to Hockley garage to work on the long cross-boundary routes to West Bromwich, Wednesbury and Dudley. Leyland Motors had offered these buses with bodies fitted with straight staircases in common with the normal BCT bodystyle. At an extra cost of only £35 per body, this was turned down by the corporation in order to obtain a quick delivery date. It was a great pity that this did not occur as the buses would have looked like the 1939 TD6C's 1270-1319 which arguably were Birmingham's most handsome-looking buses. (D. R. Harvey Collection)

2083 (Opposite, below)

The turn-back and layover point for many of the inbound bus services using the Stratford Road corridor was Mole Street. This was located between Stratford Road and a point on Highgate Road virtually opposite the bus garage. A pair of Yardley Wood garage's vehicles, both flying Coronation flags, is parked between duties. 2083 (JOJ 83), a 'New Look' front Daimler CVD6 with a Metro-Cammell body entered service in February 1951 but looks as though it was due for a repaint. It is parked in front of an exposed radiator Daimler CVD6 2003 (JOJ 3), which was some fifteen months older. Both buses have Birmingham specification Metro-Cammell bodies but the smooth curves of the concealed radiator as well as the fitting of wheel discs make the newer bus look more modern. (S. N. J. White)

2231

2231 (JOJ 231), the first of the thirty Weymann-bodied Leyland Tiger PS2/1s, which was exactly three years old to the month at the time of the Coronation, has just turned into Cartland Road, Stirchley. Photographs of these attractive and powerful single-deckers actually carrying Coronation flags are extremely rare. 2231, happily still with us as a long-time preserved Birmingham bus, is working on the long inter-suburban 27 service between West Heath, Northfield and Stirchley. It still has about two miles to go before it reaches its eastern terminus at Kings Heath. Most of these front entrance thirty-four seaters had service lives of eighteen years and with their big Leyland 0.600 engines were sometimes hired out to Midland Red to duplicate coach services to Weston-Super-Mare and Rhyl as they were a good deal faster than many of the coaches operated by local independent operators who might have been a more obvious choice for Midland Red to hire-in. (S. N. J. White)

2511

On a wet June day in 1953, similar to that of Coronation Day, 2511 (JOJ 511) is parked at the Bundy Clock in Reservoir Road, Erdington, when working on the 26-mile-long Outer Circle 11 bus service. Again carrying an advertisement, this time for the long-forgotten brand of Sportsman Cigarettes, the bus is clearly carrying the miniature Union Jack flags just below the front destination box. The bus, which had entered service on 1 September 1950 and survived until the last day of March 1969 is a Crossley DD42/6 with a very solidly-built Crossley H30/24R body. It is still in its original, 'as-built' state and retains the trafficators, hub caps and full length front wings which would be altered in future years. (A. M. Wright)

2251 (Opposite below)

Parked in front of the offices at Wellhead Lane garage in June 1953 is 2251 (JOJ 251), which is wearing the two small Coronation flags. The bus is one of the four handsome Weymann-bodied Leyland Tiger PS2/1s allocated to Perry Barr garage basically to work children special services, though they were occasionally used on short-workings on the 33 service from Kingstanding. Posing in front of the bus is Jack Thorne, who was one of the garage's fitters. 2251 would later be converted to operate as an OMO bus with the front bulkhead partially removed and an angled window built over the rear of the engine bonnet in order for the ticket machine to be mounted. This expensive and somewhat extensive rebuilding proved to be a very useful modification, allowing these buses to have their operating lives extended by about five years. (L. Deakin)

2617

The first big post-war order by BCT awarded to Guy Motors was for a modified version of their Arab III model. These were fitted with a floor-mounted Wilson pre-selector gearbox, a Gardner 8.4 litre 6LW engine and the 'New Look' concealed-radiator front. The concept for this enclosed front and bonnet had been jointly developed by BCT and Guy Motors, although Crossley 2426 was rushed into service in February 1950, some four months before the first of these 26-feet-long Guys. There were 100 of these Arab III Specials and they were bodied by Metro-Cammell. They were the last BCT buses to be built with separate lower and upper decks. 2617 (JOJ 617) was one of the last of the class, entering service on 1 May 1951, and was not withdrawn until January 1977, giving it a remarkable service life of nearly 26 years. The bus was allocated at this time to Acock's Green garage and is passing the County Ground, Edgbaston, the home of Warwickshire CC, while working on the 1A service to Acock's Green. 2617 was leaving the bus stop outside the entrance gates when Warwickshire were playing Lancashire in a three-day County Championship match which ended in a draw, though the one redeeming feature of the game was that the Lancashire off-spin bowler Roy Tattersall took 8 for 54 in the Warwickshire first innings. (S. N. J. White)

2885

Taken on the same day as the photograph of 2617, the virtually brand new 2885 (JOJ 885) stands in Edgbaston Road outside the County Ground turnstiles. Above the entrance gates is the sign showing that it would cost 2s (£0.10) to watch a whole day's County match! The bus had entered service on 1 March that year and was a Daimler CVG6 with a Crossley H30/25R body and at 27 feet 6 inches was eighteen inches longer than 2617, the Guy Arab III Special. 2885 was a Highgate Road garage bus and is working on loan to Acock's Green garage, hence the SERVICE EXTRA destination display. Behind the bus is a Vauxhall 12-4 four-door saloon car dating from April 1946. (S. N. J. White)

2836 (Opposite, below)

This Crossley-bodied Daimler CVG6, 2836 (JOJ 836), stands in Bull Street outside the red, white and blue decorated Greys department store when working on the 13A route to Yardley Wood. The bus is carrying an advertisement for Kellogg's Corn Flakes as a result of changing the contract for carrying advertisements from the tramcar fleet to the buses earlier in the year. At the beginning of June 1953, 2836 carries the pair of Coronation Union Jack flags below the front destination box which were fitted to all Birmingham City Transport buses. (G. F. Douglas)

Buses and Bunting

The Coronation was really the first celebration on a national scale since those of VE Day and VJ Day in 1945. With the country virtually bankrupt after the war, the victory seemed very difficult to bear for many. Rationing was initially even stricter than in the war; petrol was still scarce; work was there, with the desire to export in order to survive; but wages were low while inflation was high. The new Labour Government was nationalising transport, the mining and steel industries and while the National Health Service was generally recognised as a great improvement, most of the other service industries were run down and using pre-war materials. Even the weather turned against people with the winter of 1946/47 being the worst since the time of Dickens. It was a bleak period of strikes and protests culminating with the death of King George VI in February 1952. With the accession of his daughter, Queen Elizabeth II, a wave of patriotism and the promise of 'a new Elizabethan Age' swept across the country. With the impending Coronation on 2 June, flags, streamers and bunting along with patriotic slogans were put on buildings from the smallest house to the largest factories, municipal buildings and the biggest cathedrals. In Birmingham, the buses ran along such decorated streets for about two weeks before the streets and the population returned to normal.

1219

It is difficult to exactly know what this pre-war bus is actually doing as it has come down Lodge Road and is almost at the Ansell's-owned Bull's Head public house in Icknield Street while displaying the 72 route on its destination blind. It has probably 'gone round the block' from the nearby Hockley garage to take up service at Hockley Brook. What is certain is that the Coronation festivities were being celebrated in Lodge Road, with some bunting and a number of Union Jacks in evidence. The bus is 1219 (FOF 219), a Daimler COG5 with a Metro-Cammell H30/24R body which had entered service on 1 November 1939 and wasn't taken out of service until the end of April 1954. (D. R. Harvey Collection)

1319

Two former Birmingham City Transport buses with their radiators patriotically painted red, white and blue travel along a main city centre road decorated with flags and bunting. Unfortunately, this is not actually Birmingham but Bishopsgate, in the City of London. The buses were owned by Lansdowne's Luxury Coaches, Leytonstone, E11, who had acquired 1319 (FOF 319) in December 1952 and the following 240 (EOG 240) in June 1950. 1319 was the last of the fifty Leyland Titan TD6c with an attractive Leyland H28/24R body dating from November 1939 and 240 was another TD6c but with an MCCW H28/24R body which was new in February 1939. The buses are passing the premises of Harold Sims, who was a bespoke tailor with three outlets in the city. (R. Wellings)

1643

One of the unusual Park Royal-bodied AEC Regent III 0961 RT types, 1643 (GOE 643), is about to turn left in front of the Art Deco-styled Lewis's seven-storied department store, opened in 1929, from Corporation Street into Bull Street. The flags and the bunting across Corporation Street are very impressive while the huge crown and letters EIIR are just extraordinary. Long banners with St George's Cross motifs and in patriotic colours hang from Lewis's and this type of decoration was to be found throughout the city centre. The bus is working on the 32 route and is about halfway around Birmingham's then infamous one-way city centre street system. (D. R. Harvey Collection)

1831
Albert Street was an important bus terminus point and had been used as such in the past for both trams and trolleybuses, though in their case they ran in the opposite direction to the buses parked at the top of the street. This resulted in the impressive bus shelters on the right becoming redundant after several decades of use. On the right is the Beehive Store, which was the last family-owned department store in the City Centre. The street bunting was more muted than in Corporation Street, consisting of mainly Union Jacks, although somewhat strangely there is a Greek flag just above the parked buses. On 29 May 1953, just five days before the Coronation, 1831 (HOV 831), a 1948-vintage Metro-Cammell-bodied Daimler CVD6, waits at the 54 bus stop at the High Street end of the street. Parked outside the Beehive is an interesting selection of cars, including a large, black, 1937-registered Austin Eighteen owned by the City Council, a Ford V8 Pilot and a 1951-registered Morris Oxford MO. (D. R. Harvey Collection)

1833 (Opposite, above)
The wartime devastation in the Bull Ring area of the city would not be cleared away until the late 1950s and one such 'Bomb-building' site (a good old Brummie expression) is still evident behind the bus. 1833 (HOV 833), a Daimler CVD6 with a 54-seat Metro-Cammell body, is working on the 58 service to the City boundary at Sheldon and is standing on the steep hill outside the decorated Woodley's furniture store. The cobbled surface of the Bull Ring made it very slippery in wet weather and very treacherous if it was covered by snow or ice. One of the gaps caused by the wartime bombing destroyed a row of about eight shops; the café behind the bus was a temporary building dating from about 1950 that was largely constructed from reclaimed bricks. It was owned by Leo Devoti and it was there in about 1954 that your author first drank the then quite exotic Coca-Cola! (S. N. J. White)

2319
The terminus of the 1A route in Acock's Green village was outside two of the area's most important buildings; these were the 'seat of understanding', as the New Inns public house was known, and the 'seat of learning', which was Acock's Green's public library. The library, behind the bus, seems to have a somewhat tawdry length of celebratory bunting draped across the front of this 1932-constructed building. It is June 1953 and the Coronation flags on the bus have gone, leaving behind the bracket on which they were mounted that would stay on the bus until it was withdrawn in March 1964. The bus is 2319 (JOJ 319), a Crossley-bodied Crossley DD42/6 with an exposed, polished radiator. This bus was one of thirty-five Crossleys to enter service on 1 January 1950 and would spend its entire sixteen-year life operating from the nearby Acock's Green garage. (G. Burrows)

2416

New Street in the city centre was awash with flags, bunting, ribbons and Coronation motifs for
several weeks from the end of May until mid-June 1953. Around the week of Queen Elizabeth
II's Coronation, 2416 (JOJ 416), an exposed radiator Crossley DD42/6 with a Crossley
H30/24R body, has just turned out of Victoria Square into New Street as it leaves the city centre
on the 15B route to Garrett's Green Lane, to the east of the city. The suburb of Garrett's Green
had this bus route instigated on 23 November 1938, though work on the estate was suspended
throughout the war. The conductor on the bus has put the chain across the platform to show
that the bus is full-up. Until the 1990s, when it was pedestrianised, New Street was one of the
main traffic thoroughfares in central Birmingham and linked Victoria Square and the Town
Hall with the distant High Street and the Bull Ring, but in 1953, pedestrians seemed to largely
realise that pavements were for them and the road was for vehicles ... except for the women on
the left walking on the road next to the bus! (D. R. Harvey Collection)

The Coronation bunting still decorates the Co-operative shop's frontage in June 1953, almost two years after the passing of the Coventry Road trolleybuses. One of the replacement Daimler CVD6s, 2655 (JOJ 655), with a Metro-Cammell H30/24R body, and still carrying the smart wheel trims, stands near the junction with Sheaf Lane working on the 58 route. Behind is an exposed-radiator HOV-registered Daimler CVD6. The two-holed bracket mounted below the destination blind has served its patriotic purpose in the Coronation celebrations as 2655 is devoid of the two small Union Jack flags. (G. Burrows)

2861
Just about to pull away from the bus stop at the top of Snow Hill in mid-June 1953 is Crossley-bodied Daimler CVG6 2861 (JOJ 861), when it was just over six months old. The bus is working on the 29A route. This was Birmingham's second longest bus route and had the unique distinction of terminating at both ends outside the city boundary. The bus is not carrying its Coronation flags, though the buildings behind the bus are all bedecked with a wide range of Union Jacks, bunting and streamers. These buildings stood opposite the side of Snow Hill Railway Station and were all swept away in the 1960s, depriving the city of an important shopping facility. (A. M. Wright)

2596
Looking back to Birmingham's impressive Town Hall, it is noticeable that most of the street decorations are suspended over the road rather than on the buildings! Both of the Corporation buses are carrying their two Coronation flags. On the left, working on the 31A route from Gospel Lane in Acock's Green, is 2596 (JOJ 596), one of the by now nearly three year old MCCW-bodied Guy Arab III Specials which was just beginning its trip around the centre of the city on the one-way system that everyone from Birmingham understood but everyone from elsewhere didn't. The Guy has just overtaken 1593 (GOE 593), a Daimler CVG6 dating from 1947. The Daimler is being employed on the short Sandon Road service which terminated at the Bearwood boundary. (C. F. Klapper/Omnibus Society)

Buses and Trams

Throughout the first half of 1953, preparations for the abandonment of the final tram routes in Birmingham to Erdington, Short Heath and Pype Hayes took place. No sooner had Birmingham's Coronation celebrations ended than the long-standing plans were implemented for the final closure of the tram system.

The final tram and solitary trolleybus closure schemes had been finalised in 1948. Plans were originally laid out in 1939 to close the tram system, with the Washwood Heath services being the last to be withdrawn in 1944. The Second World War put these abandonments on hold until 1948, when the Stechford routes, originally earmarked for abandonment in April 1940, were finally implemented on 2 October 1948 as the first of the five-year plan of closures. The Lodge Road and Ladywood routes were closed in 1947 as they were the surviving remnants of the Dudley Road service abandonments, which closed on 30 September 1959. In the previous plan, the Erdington routes would have closed in 1943, leaving the air-brake trams to operate on the Bristol Road and Cotteridge group of routes and the final routes to go would have been the two Washwood Heath services. The 1948 plan reversed these last three closures on the grounds that the air-brake cars were, although newer, more expensive to maintain. There was also the problem of obtaining sufficient new buses to implement the extinction of electric-powered public road transport in the city. Between the first orders being places in 1946 to the last deliveries in October 1954, no less than 1,747 new buses went on to the streets of Birmingham but it was as late as 4 July 1953 before the last trams could be taken out of service for the last time.

On the final day, buses took over either in Lichfield Road at Victoria Road for inbound trams or in Steelhouse Lane, which was the city terminus. The buses were operated from Miller Street garage, from where the last trams had been operating, and the whole business of this final closure, which had begun on the Friday afternoon, was undertaken with military precision. This section is listed in chronological order.

Before the Final Tram Closure

1548

Travelling somewhat unusually in the wrong direction into the city along John Bright Street in the early months of 1953 is 1548 (GOE 548). This Daimler CVA6 has just passed the entrance to the Futurist Cinema, whose canopy stands above the pavement on the left. The bus is about to cross the junction with Severn Street. It is working on the 20 route from Weoley Castle. The bus is passing through the roadworks caused by the recent removal of the tram lines by the contractor, Cox & Danks of Langley Green. These had been used until the final abandonment of the Bristol Road and Pershore Road tram routes on 5 July 1952. (D. R. Harvey Collection)

1828
The last of the span wires in Digbeth supported the tram wires in front of the Midland Red parking area in Rea Street. This enabled the last of the Miller Street depot trams to travel across the city via the Bull Ring and through Digbeth before turning right into Rea Street. In March 1953 an SOS FEDD comes into view on the left behind the Corporation bus, 1828 (HOV 828), a Metro-Cammell-bodied Daimler CVD6 working on the 54 service from Stechford. The leading vehicle travelling out from Digbeth is a BRS-owned Austin K3 van while beyond it in the distance and just crossing the junction with Rea Street is 2075 (JOJ 75), a concealed radiator Daimler CVD6 dating from 1950. Just visible over the scrum of Corporation buses at the Rea Street junction are a large number of Midland Red double-decker buses, including a couple of rebuilt wartime vehicles, several AD2 and D5 types and, crucially, a brand new SHA-registered Leyland-bodied Titan PD2/12, classified LD8 by the company. (Birmingham Central Reference Library)

2413 (Opposite, below)
The lower part of Corporation Street had been constructed when the money to continue Joseph Chamberlain's 'Parisian boulevard' had long run out. As a result, it was lined with mid to late Victorian properties that would have been swept away had the aborted 'grand design' been implemented in the first years of Edward VII's reign. A lot of demolition did take place in the early 1930s, when the site was cleared to make way for the new Central Fire Station, opened by HRH the Duke of Kent on 2 December 1935. It was in this contrasting environment in February 1953, with civic pride on the one side of the street and run down, time expired premises on the other, that exposed radiator Crossley-bodied Crossley 2413 (JOJ 413) travels into the city from Kitts Green on a 14A service, which at this time was operated by Liverpool Street garage. Going out of 'town' is tram 698, which is on its way to Pype Hayes on the 79 route. (T. Barker)

1859

Looking in the opposite direction in Digbeth to the last photograph on Thursday 12 March 1953 shows that the positive wire for the trams going to and from Kyotts Lake Road Works was still attached to the double hangers which supported the negative wire for the Coventry Road trolleybuses, which had been abandoned at the end of June 1951. Other than the Midland Red single-deck SOS SON 2023 (DHA 641), which would be withdrawn later in the year, and the barely two-week-old LD8 4034 (SHA 434) coming out of Mill Lane, the only other identifiable bus is the Corporation Daimler CVG6 working on the 37 service from Hall Green. This is 1859 (HOV 859), dating from January 1949, which has yet to fitted, at this early stage, with Coronation flag brackets. (Birmingham Central Reference Library)

Preparing for the Tram Abandonment

2351

As the driver and conductress walk back to the depot, life goes on at Miller Street as normal. Yet the final tram abandonment was imminent and the trams, including cars 700 and 694, destined to be the final service 63 tram to Tyburn Road, await their last few weeks in service. The bus parked in the road way on the track fan is 2351 (JOJ 351), a Crossley DD42/6 with a Crossley H30/24R body, which was a visitor from the nearby Perry Barr garage. It is not fitted with Coronation flag holders and so this must have been taken in about May 1953. The conversion of Miller Street from a tram depot to a bus garage began at the end of November 1952 and trams were parked in the open air Permanent Way yard opposite the depot while about thirty trams were stabled at the reopened Witton depot. (S. N. J. White)

1721 (Opposite, below)

On Friday 26 June 1953, 1721 (HOV 721) loads up at the shelters at the Fort Dunlop factory in Holly Lane. The bus is a Leyland Titan PD2/1 with a Brush H30/24R body and it is working on the interurban 40A service to Six Ways, Aston and Lozells. This route had been introduced on 1 October 1950, when it replaced the 5 tram route. Beyond the bus is car 569, which will travel back to the city terminus in Steelhouse Lane via Tyburn Road on the 63 service. This had been the last new tram route to be opened in Birmingham, on 3 February 1930, with the 200-yard spur from Tyburn Road, whose distant junction is just beyond the distant tram on the skyline. (C. W. Routh)

3114 (Above)

Prior to entry into service, many buses were stored in the Permanent Way Yard opposite the tram depot in Miller Street in the last days of the week prior to the final tram route closures as the trams which had been parked for service in the yard were stabled for the last few days either in the main tram shed or a Witton depot. The bus facing the exit is 3114 (MOF 114), a Daimler CVG6 with a Crossley H30/25R body. On the right is a similar vehicle, in this case 3126 (MOF 126). Neither bus would remain at Miller Street garage for long, with 3114 going to Birchfield Road garage and 3126 moving to Perry Barr in about 1957. The last of these 125 Daimlers would not enter service until October 1954 and, ironically, about twenty of them were stored in the empty Witton tram shed during the summer of that year. (D. R. Harvey Collection)

1827 (Opposite, above)

After the evening rush hour had finished at 6.30 p.m. on Friday 3 July 1953, thirty-six surplus trams were driven to Kyotts Lake Road Works for storage prior to scrapping. Car 696 is about to use the cross-over in Moor Street as it had coasted down the hill in Carrs Lane from Dale End on the single line track which was only linked to the inbound track in Moor Street. On the left is bus 1827 (HOV 827), one of Coventry Road garage's many Daimler CVD6s fitted with a fifty-four-seat Metro-Cammell body. The bus is travelling into the City terminus of the 60 route in Albert Street. The recent addition of advertisements on the buses had led to small advertisements being place on the lower rear panel. This meant that the previous style of large gold fleet numbers were replaced with the smaller version that was already carried on the front lower panels. The details of each saloon's seating capacity were still carried below the rear number plate, though these would be omitted within a couple of years. (R. Grosvenor)

2069 (Opposite, below)

Travelling up the hill in Moor Street and passing the entrance to Moor Street Station is 'New Look front' Daimler CVD6 2069 (JOJ 69). It is going towards its city terminus in Albert Street when working on a 50B shortworking from Alcester Lanes End. It is the early evening of Friday 3 July 1953 as Brush-bodied 40 hp tram 664, mounted on EMB maximum traction bogies and dating from March 1924, makes its final one-way trip to Kyotts Lake Road Works, where it would be finally broken up later the same month. The BCT Inspector watches the disappearing tram and waits for the next one to coast down Carrs Lane, as there was no wiring between High Street at the top of the hill and Moor Street. Outside the Moor Street Warehouse store on the right is a Coventry-registered car dating from September 1948, but its two-door coupé body reveals nothing as to its manufacturer. (T. J. Edgington)

Buses Taking Over From Trams

3021

Still displaying the OK route number it had when it left Metro-Cammell in June 1953 and positively sparkling in the summer sunshine, 3021 (MOF 21) travels over the tram tracks in Lichfield Road on the morning of Saturday 4 July 1953 as it speeds along on its way to take up its first tram replacement duty. This bus was part of a £1m order for 125 Daimler CVG6s with Crossley bodies and 100 Metro-Cammell-bodied Guy Arab IVs, of which twenty-seven Daimlers and twenty-five Guys entered service from Miller Street garage. Just visible in the background is an unidentified tram about to complete its service life. BCT and its successor, West Midlands PTE, certainly got their money's worth from 3021 as it survived in service until October 1976. (H. Sergeant)

3032

Lined up in Sandy Lane, Aston, prior to entering service on 4 July 1953 is a row of brand new Guy Arab IVs. The leading bus is 3032 (MOF 32), while visible behind it are 3031 and 3030. All the buses in this line-up are Guy Arab IVs with 27 feet 6 inches-long Metro-Cammell bodies with a capacity of fifty-five passengers. These buses would be called up to Lichfield Road as and when they were required to take over from a tram as it arrived at Victoria Road, where it would be taken out of service and taken to Witton depot for scrapping. The Guys would remain at Miller Street until about 1963, when they were transferred to Cotteridge garage to work on the Pershore Road services. (D. R. Harvey Collection)

3033

The last of the Metro-Cammell-bodied Guy Arab IVs allocated to Miller Street from new for the change over from trams to buses was 3033 (MOF 33). It is leaving Miller Street bus garage at about 11.00 a.m. on the morning of Saturday 4 July 1953 and is being followed by two other Guys. These buses were all fitted with Gardner 6LW engines and Wilson pre-selector gearboxes with floor-mounted change levers. It is curious that the driver of 3033 is giving a hand signal rather than using his right hand trafficator. As the buses proceeded down Miller Street to Aston Road North, the final two trams, 623 and the decorated 616, were about to turn into Miller Street at the end of their final ceremonial run to Erdington. (D. S. Giles)

2301

Facing towards the city centre, Crossley-bodied Crossley DD42/6 2301 (JOJ 301) has already begun its replacement tram duties as it leaves the change over point to work into the city. On arrival in Steelhouse Lane 2301 would become the first bus to leave the city displaying the new 64 service number after car 690 had become the final tram to Erdington. Car 690 had left Steelhouse Lane at 10.42 a.m., so this photograph must have been taken about half an hour earlier. The tram passing in the opposite direction as it passes the offices of Ansells Brewery is car 541. This Brush-bodied tram, mounted on Mountain & Gibson maximum traction bogies fitted with a pair of English Electric DK30/1L 63 hp motors, had been the lowest numbered tram in the fleet since the closure of the Bristol Road group of tram routes and had entered service in early 1914. (R. Grosvenor)

2398

Strengthened Brush-bodied tram 558 has set down its last ever passengers in Lichfield Road, just short of Victoria Road, having worked in from Short Heath. After disembarking their passengers, who would then transfer to the waiting buses for the remainder of the journey into the city centre, car 558, along with some thirty-three other trams, were driven by way of Victoria Road and Park Road to Witton depot, where they would be broken up along with another eleven tramcars which were already there. The leading bus awaiting passengers from the tram is 2398 (JOJ 398), which has been put on the 65 service to Short Heath. This vehicle entered service on 1 May 1950, but differed from the earlier Crossley DD42/6s by having the more powerful and reliable Crossley downdraught engine. (R. Buckley)

2471

Destined to be one of only two Crossleys transferred and operated by West Midlands PTE (or any of the PTEs for that matter!) on 1 October 1969, 2471 (JOJ 471) was later to become the last Crossley to operate in the city, being withdrawn at the end of October 1969. The driver of 2471 receives some last minute instructions from the Inspector as passengers transfer from MRCW bogie tramcar 653 of 1923 vintage in Lichfield Road. On its other dash panel, someone had chalked the message 'Get On. Last Trip.' It is about 10.15 a.m. on Saturday 4 July 1953 and within half an hour car 653 would be arriving at Witton, where it would be broken up by W. T. Bird's scrap men. The tram had come back into Aston from Erdington and its passengers are going on to the waiting 64 route bus. (D. R. Harvey Collection)

2465

Doctors, nurses and patients stand on the balconies of the General Hospital at the bottom of Steelhouse Lane in order to get a better view of the closure of the last trio of Birmingham's tram services to Erdington when they were replaced by buses on the morning of Saturday 4 July 1953. At about 10.40 a.m., the first replacement 65 bus service to Short Heath left the Steelhouse Lane terminus. This was operated by 2465 (JOJ 465), a 'New Look front' Crossley DD42/6 with a Crossley H30/24R body. This was numerically the first of fourteen of these buses transferred to Miller Street in time for the tram abandonment. It is overtaking a parked Austin A70 police car while behind it is a Wolseley 12/48 and between 2465 and the Brush-bodied Leyland Titan PD2/1 is a late version of the 'sit-up and beg' Ford Prefect. The bus is in immaculate condition but has lost its rear wheel trims. A nice touch was that 2466 worked on the first 66 service, but the plan did not quite work as the first bus on the Erdington 64 route was 2301, an exposed radiator Crossley. (R. Knibbs)

3011

Although it entered service on 1 July 1953, 3011 (MOF 11) is carrying Coronation flag holders, suggesting that the bus had been delivered a month earlier, prior to the Coronation. This Guy Arab IV fitted with a Metro-Cammell H30/25R body has just turned out of Whittall Street into Steelhouse Lane and is hanging back from the start of the queue of intending passengers a few hours after the abandonment of the Erdington tram routes. Miller Street received brand new Guy Arab IVs 3009–3033 and Daimler CVG6s 3104–3130 for the bus take over as well as forty-nine older buses transferred from other garages. 3011 is waiting to begin a trip to Erdington and is being overtaken by a Morris-Commercial J type van. (C. Carter)

Buses But No More Trams

3009

A positively gleaming 3009 (MOF 9) has returned from Erdington on the 64A route, which was a garage-only shortworking. The bus, a Guy Arab IV with a Metro-Cammell body, is standing in Miller Street on 10 July 1953. The bus, which has been preserved since February 1976, was the first of the twenty-five of these buses to be allocated to Miller Street for the change-over from trams to buses. Only three days earlier, the last eight tramcars, stored in the tram depot as there was no room for them at Witton depot until enough trams had been broken up, had left Miller Street to go to Witton for scrapping, enabling the electric current to be finally switched off. (D. R. Harvey Collection)

3121 (Opposite, below)

With the notices informing the public of the recently implemented replacement bus services over the previous weekend, 3121 (MOF 121) is delivering its passengers in Whittall Street, which had become the inbound point for unloading the new Erdington bus services. Behind the bus is part of Birmingham's Victorian General Hospital while the newer block on the right was the nurses' home. The bus, a brand new Crossley-bodied Daimler CVG6, is working on the 64 route to Erdington which had replaced the 2 tram route. Behind it is a three-year-old Crossley DD42/6, 2300 (JOJ 300), which has come in from Short Heath on the 65 service. (S. N. J. White)

2297
Once the Erdington tram routes had been abandoned, the removal of the overhead and track was generally done with indecent haste. In September 1953, the Birmingham-based contractor Douglas was hard at work in Gravelly Hill, digging up the tram lines. The bus is an exposed-radiator Crossley DD42/6 with a Crossley H30/24R body which entered service on New Year's Day 1950. It is working on the 64 service, this having replaced the 2 tram route to Erdington on 4 July 1953. This replacement bus service terminated at the old tram terminus at the row of shops just beyond Chester Road. Many of the new bus services were extended to a new terminus in order to serve areas developed after the tram route was opened but this was not possible at Erdington as the terminus was within yards of the city boundary. (R. Knibbs)

2406 (Opposite, above)
The tram overhead has gone but the tram tracks in Aston Road North still remain on Tuesday 10 November 1953. In the background is Aston Cross and towering over it is the impressive Ansells Brewery building, which dated from the 1930s. Here the smell of brewing beer and the odours coming from the HP Sauce factory mingled in the air in a most mouth-watering way. 2406 (JOJ 406), one of the thirty downdraught-engined Crossley DD42/6s with Crossley H30/24R body, dating from 1 May 1950, has just left the bus stop and has to pull out in order to overtake a 1937-registered Wolseley Series III 12/48 saloon. The bus is working on an inbound 66 service from Pype Hayes and is about to pass the Astoria Cinema.

The Theatre Royal, Aston, was built at a cost of £6,500 and opened on 7 August 1893. The theatre closed for live entertainment in 1926 and was converted for cinema use, reopening as the Astoria Cinema on 12 December 1927. Only two years after this photograph was taken, on 26 November 1955, the Astoria closed as a cinema and the building was converted into a television studio for ATV and ABC Television Limited, and renamed the Alpha Television Studios, opening on 17 February 1956. Eventually it became the home of television programmes such as *Ready, Steady, Go!*, to which the author went to cheer on the latest 1960s pop songs or group, and of course the awful soap *Crossroads*, famous for its fluffed lines, collapsing sets and total lack of continuity – it was wonderfully bad! (Birmingham City Engineers Dept.)

3113

Standing at the former Erdington tram terminus of the 64 bus service, with the Yenton public house and the Chester Road junction hidden by the trees on the right, is 3113 (MOF 113), a Crossley-bodied Daimler. It is September 1953 and by this time the tram tracks have gone and the tram lay-by has been converted into a bus turning circle. On the other side of the road is another one of the same type, waiting to leave for the city centre. While the Daimler CVG6s were fitted with the reliable Gardner 6LW 8.4 litre diesel engine, they were an altogether much more refined and quieter vehicle than the Guys, which always seemed to be an altogether more solid, powerful, but noisier, bus. (R. Knibbs)

Buses in the City Centre During Coronation Year

A quick spin around Birmingham buses during 1953 shows a wide range of the types of buses that were being operated by Birmingham City Transport, although by this time pre-war buses were noticeably thin on the ground and all the war-time buses with MoS specification, such as Daimler CWA6s and Guy Arabs, had been sold.

1323

Pulling away from the Colmore Row shelters is the last of the quartet of 8-foot-wide Daimler COG6s that were intended for Johannesburg in South Africa, but were not sent due to the danger of German U-boat activity in the Atlantic Ocean. 1323 (FVP 923) entered service from Yardley Wood garage on 14 March 1942 and was painted all-over grey. The four buses were banished to working on the suburban 18 service between Yardley Wood and Northfield due to them being over the regulation width by six inches and also being subjected to height restrictions. In 1946 they were transferred to Harborne garage, and then to the newly opened Quinton garage in 1950, and at both bases they operated on the service which basically only entailed running along the wide and straight Hagley Road. (R. Hannay)

296

The conductor stands on the back platform of the prototype Leyland Titan PD2, 296 (HOJ 396), in the autumn of 1953. He has his Ultimate ticket machine ready for action but as there are no passengers on the bus, it is between duties. It is a good job that he is a tall gentleman as the platform bell push on the Leyland body was very high and awkwardly placed for anyone of below average height. As a result, the allocation of conductresses working a duty on 296 was very rare. 296 was the second of only two PD2s to be built but unlike CVA 430, which was broken up in 1951, this Birmingham vehicle was as good as the day it was built when it was withdrawn in October 1967 after twenty years' service. The bus is in Bull Street and has crossed the road from the stop outside Grey's Department store in order to turn right into Steelhouse Lane, the scene of the final tram departures in Birmingham just a few months earlier. (D. Williams)

1666

Standing at the stop at the top of Snow Hill on Thursday 8 January 1953 when working on the cross-city 29A route is 1666 (HOV 666). This Brush-bodied Leyland Titan PD2/1 is facing the entrance to Bull Street, but as this was one-way against the bus, 1666 would turn left into Steelhouse Lane and go via Corporation Place, Stafford Street and Dale End before reaching High Street, from where it would begin its run out along Stratford Road to the terminus on the Hall Green/Solihull boundary. If passengers stood on the right where the railings and bus stop are, they could look at the trains through the open spaces in the wall of Snow Hill station where, with the wind in the right direction, they might well be enveloped by smoke from an outgoing locomotive. (Birmingham City Engineers Dept.)

2658 (Opposite, below)

On the other side of Snow Hill Station was Livery Street. It was here that the buses coming in from the Soho Road and starting beyond the city from West Bromwich, Wednesbury, Great Bridge and Dudley all terminated. Standing at the unloading stop just above the taxi entrance to the station in Livery Street just short of Colmore Row is 2658 (JOJ 658), a Daimler CVD6 with a Metro-Cammell H30/24R body which entered service on 1 July 1951 from Coventry Road, where it was used as a trolleybus replacement vehicle. By now allocated to Hockley garage, the bus is being employed on the 69 service from Lozells. This class of 150 buses were the last half-cab Daimlers to be bodied by Metro-Cammell for Birmingham City Transport. (A. M. Wright)

1097

The Soho Road services entered the city via Livery Street and picked up passengers in Colmore Row in front of the main entrance to Snow Hill Station. This is where pre-war Daimler COG5 1097 (CVP 197) is standing and is waiting to leave with its load of passengers on the 72 service to the city boundary with West Bromwich at The Hawthorns. It will immediately turn left into the steep descent of Snow Hill, having gone around three sides of the former GWR mainline station. 1097 had entered service on 6 October 1937 and received its second replacement body in March 1949. This body was a stylish English Electric H28/26R intended for Manchester Corporation, twenty of which were bought by BCT in 1941 after their original new Daimler chassis were destroyed in the air-raid on Coventry on 14 November 1940. This body had originally been fitted to bus 820 (BOP 820) and survived on 1097 until the bus was withdrawn at the end of May 1954. (D. R. Harvey Collection)

2435

On Sunday 24 May 1953, which was obviously a warm day as the driver's windscreen has been opened while most of the saloon ventilators have been opened as well, a 'New Look front' Crossley-bodied Crossley DD42/6 stands at the 14 route terminus in Old Square facing Corporation Street outside Crane's music shop. Old Square had been the last of Birmingham's Georgian town squares to be redeveloped in the 1880s. These late nineteenth century buildings behind the bus would survive for another ten years before being demolished themselves. In 1953 the 14 group of services was operated by Liverpool Street garage, which they would continue to do until April 1955, when they were transferred to the newly opened Lea Hall garage. The bus, sans advertisements, has been fitted with Coronation flag holders. The impeccable appearance of the bus, 2435 (JOJ 435), is slightly spoilt by it not having hub caps on the rear wheels. (J. C. Gillham)

1494
Climbing up the Bull Ring in the autumn of 1953 is 1494 (GOE 494). This Daimler CVA6
was fitted with a Metro-Cammell H30/24R body and dated from July 1947. It is working on
the cross-city 29A service to Kingstanding and the Pheasey Estate and will continue straight
up the hill and turn into New Street. These buses were fitted with the small AEC 7.57 litre
engine and, although weighing only 7 tons 12 cwt, were slightly underpowered and with a full
load such as being carried by 1494 did labour a bit on the steep hill of the cobbled Bull Ring.
The advertisement above the entrance of Campbell's furniture shop rather said it all when it
proclaimed it was 'Tumbling Down' as the front of their building was propped up with huge
wooden props and the hoardings concealing a derelict bomb site on the corner of Park Street.
(R. Hannay)

639 (Opposite, below)
The only four bay construction bodies to be built after the war for BCT were the Park Royal
ones mounted on the RT type AEC Regent III chassis. The demonstration of London Transport's
RT 19 in June and July 1941 resulted in a provisional order for the Regent, to be delivered after
hostilities had ended. The result was fifteen buses built on a fairly standard Park Royal frame
but with the requirements of BCT added as almost an afterthought. These design peculiarities
included the long angled windscreen (to reduce glare and reflections) and BCT's standard
internal fixtures and fittings. The result was both weird and attractive at the same time. The
batch was numbered 1631 to 1645 and was delivered between June and October 1947 and all
were allocated to Acock's Green garage. In the summer of 1953, 1639 (GOE 639), dating from 1
September 1947, waits at the Bull Ring stop with evidence of the devastation after the wartime
bombing raids behind. This was the first stop after the Albert Street terminus for the 44A service
to Lincoln Road North in Acock's Green. (E. Surfleet)

2894

Turning into Moor Street from the war-battered Bull Ring in the autumn of 1953 is 2894 (JOJ 894). The bus is working on the long 37 service from Hall Green, which would terminate in the nearby Albert Street. 2894 had entered service in May 1953, operating from Highgate Road garage, remaining there until the garage closed in July 1962. These Daimler CVG6s were fine buses and if their Crossley bodies were not quite as robust as their Metro-Cammell contemporaries, they had in some cases very long lives, though 2894 was one of the first to be withdrawn by West Midlands PTE, going in November 1971. (R. Hannay)

2216

About to travel to its city terminus in Paradise Street in the spring of 1953 is 2216 (JOJ 216). This Leyland Titan PD2/1 with Park Royal H29/25R bodywork is standing outside the impressive Museum and Art Gallery in Chamberlain Square. The bus is working on the 95 service to Ladywood whose route took it in a large arc via Holloway Head, Five Ways and Icknield Port Road to terminate opposite Dudley Road Hospital, which was only just over one mile from where it started! This fifty-strong class of buses had attractive looking, non-standard Birmingham five-bay construction bodies, which had a family resemblance to the 1947 AEC RT buses. The class was split between Hockley and Rosebery Street garages, but with their fast turn of speed, always seemed wasted on the short Ladywood route. (S. N. J. White)

3001 (Opposite, below)

In Victoria Square, the experimental lightweight bodied Guy Arab IV 3001 (LOG 301) is working on the 31A service to the Gospel Lane Loop in Acock's Green. It is standing outside the offices of the Canadian Pacific Railway with the Waterloo Street junction behind it. This bus had a Saunders-Roe alloy-construction body, but careful design work by the Beaumaris-based company had produced a body which externally at least was a very good copy of a standard BCT bus. The bus weighed in at 7 tons 4½ cwt and at this time in the spring of 1953 still had a Gardner 6LW engine, which would have made the bus something of a 'flier'. By June 1953 the engine was replaced by a Gardner 5LW unit, to the disappointment of 'all who rode on her'. (D. R. Harvey Collection)

2261
One of the delights of the original New Street Station was the road between the two halves of the station. Most passengers would not have been aware that the half on the right was originally the old L&NWR, while on the left was the later Midland Railway station. The road was named Queen's Drive and served as an approach road for railway lorries, taxis and private car access. With the advertisement for the local Davenports beers above it, 2261 (JOJ 261), the first of the five Leyland Olympic HR40 with a Weymann B36F body stands somewhat hopefully waiting for passengers who might wish to use the service to Elmdon Airport. It was a 1953 version of the Airport Transfer service. These underfloor-engined Leylands were some of the first of the type to operate in the UK, but as they were ordered before the Construction & Use Regulations were altered, they were built to the old short 27 foot 6 inch length. (S. N. J. White)

1030 (Opposite, above)
Alongside New Street Station, on the old Midland Railway side of the station, was the appropriately named Station Street. It had been used as a tram terminus since the Edwardian period and subsequently was used as an alternative bus terminus to more central sites in the city such as High Street and Albert Street. It was also used as a terminus for some of the recent abandoned Coventry Road trolleybus services. The top end of Station Street was used mainly by Midland Red bus routes, but the Hill Street end behind this bus was the preserve of the Corporation buses. In April 1953, a rather smart-looking 1030 (CVP 130), a Metro-Cammell-bodied Daimler COG5 dating from August 1937, is working on the 46 service to Hall Green, which was a remnant of the pre-1937 Stratford Road tram services; this bus route was suspended in August 1958, while the long-lived COG5 would survive until 1960. (R. Knibbs)

3000

One of the busiest termini, near to New Street Station, was that in Navigation Street. Buses, which had only replaced the trams on 5 July 1952, ran from here to Selly Oak, Northfield, Longbridge and Rednal or Rubery, or as in this case by way of Pershore Road to Cotteridge. 3000 (LOG 300) was the last of the 100 Guy Arab IV 6LWs, of which the first ones were used for the Bristol and Pershore Road tram services, entering service on 1 January 1953. The last six, 2995–3000, were fitted with constant mesh gearboxes which made them somewhat difficult to drive. 3000 is working on the 45C shortworking route to Kings Norton during the period just after the Coronation, but its sojourn at Cotteridge was brief as it would soon be transferred to Washwood Heath garage. (D. R. Harvey Collection)

Around the Suburbs by Bus in Coronation Year

A journey around the suburbs in Coronation year showing Birmingham City Transport buses at various locations reveals that the bus fleet was kept in excellent condition. In fact, their dignified dark blue and cream livery brightened up the still somewhat drab, early post-war suburbia which in 1953 still had swathes of Victorian terraced housing and an industrial inner heartland. Towards the outer areas, there were huge areas of interwar council housing as well as industrialised suburbs such as Longbridge, Erdington and the River Tame Valley and Tile Cross.

123

With the remnants of the winter's snow on the pavements and slush in the gutters, a Daimler COG5 waits in Waverley Road, Small Heath, at the clocking-in point of the 28A service. On Monday 9 February 1953, this Metro-Cammell-bodied veteran, 123 (EOG 123), dating from 1938, stands with its engine switched off waiting for its allotted time to depart. Meanwhile its passengers try to keep warm as best as they can as Birmingham buses, although extremely well-appointed, did not have the luxury of heaters. Behind the bus is one of the many rows of late Victorian houses built at the end of the nineteenth century which were a distinct improvement on the previous tunnel-backs, which had neither the luxury of bay windows nor small front gardens as they opened directly on to the street. (J. Cull)

2599 (Opposite, below)

Just before the Coronation celebrations, 2599 (JOJ 599), a 26-feet-long Guy Arab III Special with a fifty-four-seat MCCW body, is about to be overtaken by a Morris Oxford MO car. The bus is passing Edward Major's butchers shop in Camp Hill and is working on the 44A route to Lincoln Road North. The driver is carefully trying to avoid both the granite sets and the tram lines in order to give a better ride to his passengers. This section of Camp Hill was still wired up for trams going to and from Kyotts Lake Road Works, located in Sparkbrook about half a mile away, off the nearby Stratford Road. Increasingly, the trams would be making a one-way trip to the works as the date of the abandonment neared. (S. N. J. White)

2713

One of Liverpool Street garage's operations was a large contribution to the Inner Circle route. One of their buses, 2713 (JOJ 713), a Metro-Cammell-bodied Daimler CVD6 dating from September 1951, is parked alongside the Bundy Clock in Highgate Road outside the mock-Tudor Brewer's Arms public house in August 1953. If the bus was running early, the wait here could be quite long, but if the bus was running late, the driver would stop, switch off, get out of the cab, run round to the clock and peg-in with his key. Then back to the bus, pressing the starter button before his feet had left the ground and in these preselector Daimlers, move the gear quadrant to first gear position, press the select pedal, release the handbrake and pull out and be on his way. The whole episode was like a Grand Prix pit stop, such was the speed at which these expert drivers could operate! (S. N. J. White)

2989
Guy Arab IV 2989 (JOJ 989) has just passed Walford Road as it pulls up to the bus shelters in Stratford Road, on the Sparkbrook/Sparkhill boundary outside Wassall's shoe shop. This Metro-Cammell-bodied bus was just 25 days older than the Daimler CVG6 in the following photograph and is working on an outbound 32 service to Gospel Lane in the Acock's Green/Hall Green area. The Guy was one of many of the class allocated to Acock's Green garage which would spend most of their operational lives at that garage. (S. N. J. White)

2885
Turning from the Hall Green tram terminus in 1953 across the former tramway central reservation is one of Highgate Road garage's Crossley-bodied Daimler CVG6s. 2885 (JOJ 885) is working on the 46 route. This bus service was introduced on 6 January 1937 as a direct replacement for the 18 tram route, which served the wholesale markets in the Jamaica Row area of the city. The route terminated in Station Street. With a declining need for the service, it was withdrawn on 16 August 1958. 2885 is the only 'New Look' front Daimler CVG6, as waiting just short of the terminus in Stratford Road are three exposed-radiator examples, dating from 1949 and fitted with Metro-Cammell bodies. (W. A. Camwell)

2890 (Opposite, below)
Waiting for a replacement driver to arrive from the nearby Highgate Road garage outside the splendid Houses bakery shop in Stratford Road, Sparkbrook, is 2890 (JOJ 890). Behind the bus is a row of 1880s shops in Stratford Road, built at the time that the area was developed. Beyond the telephone box is Walford Road, where the Inner Circle crossed Stratford Road before it headed off towards the BSA factory in Small Heath. One of the roads which crossed Walford Road was Osborn Road; No. 152 was the home of the young Sid Field (1 April 1904 – 3 February 1950), one of the great British comedians, who died when on the verge of 'the big time' at the tragically early age of 45. Entering service on 25 March 1953, this Crossley-bodied 'New Look front' Daimler CVG6 was therefore only a few months old when it was working on the 37 service to the City boundary in Hall Green. The Crossley body differed slightly when compared to the contemporary Metro-Cammell body on the next class of Guy Arab IV buses. The cream band below the destination box on the Crossley bodies was narrower, while the cab door was slightly wider. Also on the rear dome, the khaki roof on the Crossley bodies was separated from the cream by a thin black livery band. (S. N. J. White)

2097
The Warstock area of Yardley Wood was developed in the mid-1920s as a municipal housing estate and was reached by the 24 bus service on 19 November 1930. Standing at the terminus of the 24 route at Arlington Road in August 1953 is 2097 (JOJ 97), a Metro-Cammell-bodied Daimler CVD6, which had entered service on 1 March 1951 from Yardley Wood garage and spent its entire working life at the garage, not being withdrawn until September 1966. These buses were ordered in 1947 but their construction was delayed at Metro-Cammell. The result was that the delivery of these 'New Look front' buses was very protracted, starting in September 1950 and not being completed until August 1951. Daimler-engined buses were always very quiet and smooth to both drive and ride in but they were heavy on engine oil and were difficult for engine fitters to work on. (D. R. Harvey Collection)

1121 (Opposite, above)
Not only did the 1A route serve the Warwickshire County Ground in Edgbaston Road but also the famous 250-acre Cannon Hill Park. The land for the park had been donated by Miss Louisa Ann Ryland (1814–89) in April 1873, She was a Victorian philanthropist and this lovely park now consists of formal, conservation, woodland and sports areas as well as a boating lake, bowling greens, tennis courts and picnic areas. The queue are waiting to board 1121 (CVP 221), a 1937 Daimler COG5 which by this time had been fitted with its second Metro-Cammell body, which came from bus 1024. The bus is working towards Five Ways and the city centre on a warm summer's day as the driver has his windscreen open. (D. R. Harvey Collection)

3137

Standing in Acock's Green village in front of the 1920s shops is 3137 (MOF 137). This Crossley-bodied Daimler CVG6 was one of the first new vehicles to be delivered after the large influx for the Erdington tramway abandonment, entering service on 1 September 1953. The bus was allocated to Acock's Green garage when new but it was soon transferred to Miller Street garage. 3137 was a very good investment as it remained in service with WMPTE until December 1976. The bus is on an inbound 44A service and looks very smart with the original full-length front wings, hub-caps (known locally as dustbin lids) and trafficators. The bus, having entered service after the Coronation, is not fitted with the small flag holder brackets. (S. E. Letts)

2592

The 32 terminus was in Gospel Lane, Acock's Green, and was worked anticlockwise in conjunction with the 31A route. Buses were introduced on 1 January 1936 to service this large area of municipal housing. In August 1953, a pair of Guy Arab III Specials stand at the terminus, the leading one being 2592 (JOJ 592), which had entered service on 1 February 1951. These buses, of which there were one hundred, were specially designed by Guy Motors to the requirements of BCT and had such chassis modifications as having no rear platform extension, automatic chassis lubrication, a Wilson pre-selector gearbox and fluid flywheel, an offside mounted fuel tank and of course the 'New Look front', which concealed the radiator with a stylish cowling and bonnet with integrated full length wings. (G. Burrows)

1767

Around the corner from Yardley Road, with the other side of Collier's car showroom and garage behind the buses, was the former cobbled Yardley trolleybus turning circle. This was used by the replacement Coventry Road bus services which were introduced on 1 July 1951. Just over two years later on Thursday 23 July 1953, on the day that the film *Gentlemen Prefer Blondes* was released, starring Marilyn Monroe and Jane Russell, a less historical event was taking place at Yardley. 1767 (HOV 767), a Daimler CVD6 with a Metro-Cammell body, dating from March 1948, waits to leave on the peak hour-only 57B service to Station Street. This had replaced the 57 trolleybus route but, like so many bus routes which went to Station Street, the route was abandoned, in this case on 21 March 1961. The bus standing behind is 1986 (HOV 986), which first entered service on 1 November 1949, working on the 60 service from Crane's Park Estate. Although these two buses looked the same, 1767 had the uppern saloon passenger handrail mounted across the front windows whereas 1986, a year new, had the handrail placed in the later standard position below the windows at the front. (G. F. Douglas, courtesy A. D. Packer)

873 (Opposite, below)

On Thursday 28 May 1953, with a string of early Coronation bunting strung from the telegraph pole on the left, pre-war Daimler COG5 873 (BOP 873) stands at the bus stop in Yardley Road when working on the Outer Circle 11 route. This stop was opposite the Swan public house, Yardley, and the bus is facing the junction with Coventry Road. The building behind the bus is Collier's car showroom and garage, part of which was the former City of Birmingham Tramways depot, which was closed when the company's operation of tramcars ceased on New Year's Eve 1912. 873, despite it having a long life, was not part of the extensive body swapping and renovation programme that involved over five hundred COG5 buses. It entered service on 1 August 1936 and was withdrawn at the end of January 1954 whereupon it was converted into a snowplough, surviving for another nine years. (J. Cull)

1848 (Above)
On 23 July 1953, 1848 (HOV
848), a Daimler CVG6 dating from
December 1948, crosses Bordesley
Green East, Stechford, on 23
July 1953. This had been the last
tramway extension in Birmingham,
having opened on
26 August 1928 from Belcher's
Lane along the reserved track to
Stuarts Road. 1848 has come out
of Richmond Road when working
on the 36 route, having just left
the terminus. The 36 route was
extremely busy in the peak periods,
serving the industrial areas of
Tyseley and Hay Mills, but as seen
here, was poorly patronized during
the rest of the day. These Daimler
CVG6s had Metro-Cammell-
bodies, which had a capacity for
fifty-four passengers. They weighed
7 tons 17 cwt and were excellent,
hard working buses, mainly
being used on routes operated
by Highgate Road and Liverpool
Street garages. (G. F. Douglas,
courtesy A. D. Packer)

1324
The first of the 'unfrozen' Leyland Titan TD7s, 1324 (FON 324), is about to cross the Birmingham & Fazeley Canal as it leaves the Fort Dunlop factory in Holly Lane on 30 June 1953. It is working on the peak hours-only 40 service to Lozells via Gravelly Hill. As Birmingham was given no choice in the selection of vehicles, it was operating buses with a full fifty-six-seat capacity, in this case with a Leyland body. 1324 was delivered on 24 February 1942 with grey paintwork and was allocated to Perry Barr Garage for its entire career. These attractive buses were not particularly liked by the drivers as they had very slow gear changes, which could be improved upon if the clutch stop was used, but they were hard work! As a result of this, they were mainly used on longer routes where gear changes were at a minimum. (D. R. Harvey Collection)

2698 (Opposite, below)
The driver of 2698 (JOJ 698) poses in front of his charge at the 56B shortworking terminus opposite the Fox & Goose public house in Washwood Heath Road at the junction with Stechford Lane in September 1953. The mock-Tudor building on the right is the Beaufort Cinema. When it was opened on 4 August 1929 it was outside the Birmingham boundary and it came under the control of Meriden Council and as a consequence it was granted a Sunday license when all of the cinemas in Birmingham only opened Monday to Saturday. The 56B was the direct replacement of the 10 tram service, which loaded up in the central reservation just visible on the left. 2698 is a Daimler CVD6 with a Metro-Cammell body which was about two years old at this time. (D. R. Harvey Collection)

2108

The normal daytime service to Lozells was the 40A route, which terminated at Gravelly Hill, though more accurately it was at Salford Bridge. Today this section of road does not exist as it is underneath what is colloquially known as 'Spaghetti Junction' on the M6 motorway. Standing at the Bundy Clock waiting to leave for Lozells on 15 May 1953 is one of Perry Barr garage's Daimler CVD6s, 2108 (JOJ 108), fitted with a Metro-Cammell H30/2R body and a fortnight shy of being two years old. The bus is carrying both Coronation flag holders and advertisements, with the one on the nearside for Hercules bicycles, which were made locally in Rocky Lane, Aston. By the end of the 1930s, Hercules had produced more than six million bicycles and could claim to be the biggest manufacturer of cycles in the world. In the 1950s Hercules had become one of the largest businesses in Aston and to this day, the mascot of Aston Villa football club is Hercules the Lion. (J. C. Gillham)

1396
Parked in front of a 'New Look front' Crossley in Miller Street is FOP 396. This bus superficially looks normal enough, though in reality it was very different as in this state, despite having a full set of seats, it never carried a passenger! The bus, by now numbered 96 in the service fleet, was originally built as a Park Royal-bodied Guy Arab II and entered service on 25 March 1944 as bus number 1396. Withdrawn on New Year's Eve 1950, the bus received a 1943 Brush MoS body which had originally been fitted to a 1930 AEC Regent 661, 398 (OG 398). This Brush body had then been put on to another Regent, 416, in May 1948 and converted to a dual control trainer, with the instructor sitting behind the cab having a separate steering wheel, handbrake, and foot controls. The body and dual control equipment were then fitted on 1 May 1952 to the recently withdrawn 1396. Always displaying SPECIAL in the destination box, 96 survived until January 1968, latterly converted to open-top for use as a tree-lopper. (D. R. Harvey Collection)

2873 (Opposite, below)
In March 1953, 2873 (JOJ 873), a Crossley-bodied Daimler CVG6, is about to do duty on a Villa Park Special and has yet to leave the vicinity of its home garage in Highgate Road, which is behind the bus. It is parked outside the premises of Harper, Preston & Bedworth, who were jig and pressed tool makers based in Stoney Lane. It was quite common for a number of garages to have turns on the local football specials and all buses fitted with triple indicator destination boxes had ST ANDREWS, VILLA PARK and THE HAWTHORNS on the blind irrespective of their garages' specific blinds for the routes they operated. (D. R. Harvey Collection)

2117

Being employed on an Outer Circle shortworking in Bromford Lane, Erdington, is 2117 (JOJ 117). This is a 'New Look front' Metro-Cammell-bodied Daimler CVD6 and is working back to Perry Barr, after it will return to that suburb's BCT garage. With the distant tram wires serving the 79 tram route in Tyburn Road still intact, this suggests that this is June 1953. The bus is lacking the rear hub caps, which gradually became an increasing problem which eventually resulted in them being removed. The hub caps tended to make the brakes run hot and fade, but several hub caps came off speeding buses and had the effect of a Boadicean chariot. (G. Burrows)

2489
Crossley-bodied Crossley DD42/6 2489 (JOJ 489) waits alongside the Kings Head public house, built in 1905, in Lordswood Road in June 1953. The bus, already fitted with Coronation flag holders, is working on the Outer Circle 11 route and is within sight of Bearwood Road's shopping centre just over the city boundary and the bus station, being separated from them by Hagley Road. The crew are waiting at the Bundy Clock to 'peg-the-clock' when their departure time has come round. The fifty-four-seat bus, very solidly built at 8 tons 6 cwt 2 qtrs, entered service on 1 July 1950 from the nearby Harborne garage and remained in service until 31 March 1969, despite having a four-speed synchromesh gearbox rather than the pre-selector gearboxes fitted to Daimlers and Guys, which were generally more popular with the drivers. 2489 has been preserved in this pristine condition by the author of this book. (G. Burrows)

1312 (Opposite, below)
Leaving Bearwood Bus Station in February 1953 is 1312 (FOF 312). The bus is working on the B82 service back to Birmingham via Cape Hill and Dudley Road. This route was the direct successor to the 29 tram route, which had its terminus in Bearwood Road, only yards from the junction with Hagley Road. A problem with loading the replacement buses in the street was a contributory factor to the opening of Bearwood Bus Station in February 1952. 1312, a Leyland-bodied Leyland Titan TD6c, was one of the last seven of the fifty buses numbered 1270–1319 to enter service in November 1939, but after an operating life working from Hockley and the Rosebery Street garage was by now in its last few months of service. It was withdrawn at the end of October 1953 but remained in store for over a year before being sold to Lloyds of Nuneaton. (D. R. Harvey Collection)

3129
Delivered to Miller Street garage in time for the final tram abandonment on 4 July 1953, 3129 (MOF 129) is a Daimler CVG6 with a Crossley H30/25R body. Displaying that archetypal BCT SERVICE EXTRA destination, it is working on an Outer Circle shortworking. Buses with the triple indicator number blind layout rarely showed a route number when being used on a route not covered by that garage's destination blinds. 3129 is standing in Aston Lane near to the distant Witton Square at the bus stop outside Frank Jolly's electrical supplies shop. The distant exposed radiator Crossley is waiting at the 39 route terminus in Witton Lane adjacent to the former Witton tram depot, which for over twenty years until 2011 was the home of the Aston Manor Bus Museum. (R. H. G. Simpson)

1109

Parked in Oxhill Road opposite the Uplands public house in August 1953 are two pre-war buses, both with Metro-Cammell bodywork. The leading bus is 1109 (CVP 209), a Daimler COG5 dating from 1 November 1937 which is going back to Harborne garage. Behind it is one of the eighty-five Leyland Titan TD6cs, 242 (EOG 242), which is working on the 70 service. 242 was one of the buses that briefly operated from Acock's Green garage for a couple of months before the Hockley tram conversion. These buses had torque convertor gearboxes which were easy to use by former tramcar drivers, but they were less economical than the Daimler COG5s. They also sat two less, with only twenty-eight seats in the upper saloon as they were too heavy with the torque convertors to pass the unladen weight test. (D. R. Harvey Collection)

2171 (Opposite, below)

Hockley garage was always associated with Leyland buses with the pre-war torque convertor Leyland Titan TD6cs with both Metro-Cammell and Leyland bodywork being at the garage to open the new Soho Road bus services after the abandonment of the trams on that route on 1 April 1939. The post-war bus fleet consisted of all the 1949 Leyland-bodied Leyland Titan PD2/1s as well as the first fifteen of the Park Royal-bodied PD2/1s. In late 1953, three of these types are in attendance inside Hockley garage. On the right with the radiator muff is 2195 (JOJ 195), one of the Park Royal-bodied buses which were incorrectly fitted out by the coachbuilders with a straight blue band at the front and the destination box set too high. Next to it is 2171 (JOJ 171), one of the all-Leyland buses, and at the far end 1314 (FOF 314), one of the fifty TD6cs with attractive Leyland H28/24R bodywork which had entered service on 1 November 1939. After withdrawal at the end of December 1953, it was exported to Cyprus by Kallis Lefkaritis, who removed the top deck and ran it in the Larnaca area. (D. Williams)

293

The bus service along Soho Road as far as the City boundary at the Hawthorns, home of West Bromwich Albion, was numbered 72. Working on this route, near to Grove Lane, is 293 (EOG 293). This Leyland Titan TD6c had its original Metro-Cammell body destroyed on the night of 22 November 1940 when Hockley garage was bombed. The bus had been rebodied with an English Electric H28/26R body which had been intended for Manchester Corporation, hence the curvaceous livery, reflecting its original operator's streamlined red and white paint style. Just visible on the bulkhead is the torque convertor header tank which lubricated the gearbox with a paraffin and oil mixture. The bus was due to be shortly withdrawn and was taken out of service on 31 January 1954. (D. Barlow)

2531 (Opposite, below)

On 27 September 1953, 2531 (JOJ 531) is parked in Ridgacre Road at its junction with Ridgacre Lane, which is the road on the left. This was the terminus of the 3A route from 18 December 1949 until 15 January 1961, when it was extended again to Quinton Road West via Ridgacre Lane. The bus is standing outside the 1930s row of shops and is facing Quinton bus garage. This Guy Arab III Special had a Metro-Cammell H30/24R body and entered service from Quinton garage on 8 August 1950 and stayed at there until 1964, when it was transferred to Selly Oak garage. Guys were the backbone of the original Quinton garage fleet, with approximately thirty-five of the type allocated there. (B. W. Ware)

2150
The terminus of the long 74 bus route between Birmingham and Dudley was in Birmingham Road at the bottom of Castle Hill. Empty buses used to pull up short of the terminus at Midland Red's Dudley garage in order that their crews might get a cup of tea or use the garage toilets. A pair of Leyland-bodied Leyland Titan PD2/1s, 2150 and 2148, are parked outside Dudley garage during 1953. On the left is 2363 (FHA 867), a Midland Red SOS FEDD with a Brush forward entrance body probably working on the B87 service back to Birmingham via Oldbury. The two BCT Leylands will shortly go to the traffic island about fifty yards beyond the garage and then climb Castle Hill, passing the entrance to Dudley Zoo before reaching Dudley Bus Station in Fisher Street. (E. Chitham)

3008
A very well loaded, brand new Guy Arab IV is stopped in Hagley Road West as it unloads some of its passengers in July 1953. The bus is working out of the city on the 9 route to Quinton city boundary. This bus was one of only five of the class which entered service on 1 May 1953 from Quinton garage rather than those which were first licensed two months later for the Erdington tram abandonment. These 27 feet 6 inches-long buses had fifty-five seats and were well equipped, though economies had been taken in the body specification with more leather cloth rather than moquette in the lower saloon. However, they did look extremely smart when new. (D. Griffiths)

3003
The driver of the first of the MOF-registered Guy Arab IVs with Metro-Cammell H30/25R bodies poses in front of his gleaming, brand new bus. 3003 (MOF 3) entered service on 1 May 1953 and is so new that it has yet to be fitted with the Coronation flag holders. 3003 is parked at the Quinton terminus of the 9 route just off Hagley Road West in Ridgacre Road. Although not in this pristine state, 3003 survived until the very end of West Midlands PTE's operation of what were latterly somewhat euphemistically called 'Birmingham Standards'. (D. R. Harvey Collection)

1917
With snow on the ground in December 1953, 1917 (HOV 917) stands alongside the wall of Rubery Hill Hospital. It is waiting to return to the city centre on the 63 route. The bus is a Daimler CVG6 with a Metro-Cammell body and dated from June 1949. A small number of these buses were allocated to Selly Oak garage around the time of the Bristol Road tram conversions, but by 1954 this bus had been transferred to Liverpool Street garage. The driver of 1917 would have been better off in the cold weather than his conductor as he had the advantage of a warm Gardner 6LW engine alongside him whereas his conductor had to stand on the open back platform. (D. R. Harvey Collection)

2037
Parked outside the Rose & Crown in Rubery on 1 May 1953 is a type of Corporation bus not usually associated with the Bristol Road routes. 2037 (JOJ 37), which by chance had the earliest chassis number of this batch of 'New Look front' buses, was a Daimler CVD6 with a Metro-Cammell body that was very similar to the same manufacturer's product on the 2526 class of Guy Arab III Specials. The batch of 100 buses ran from 2031–2130, but their construction was severely delayed at the body builders and so the first members of the class, including 2037, did not enter service until November 1950, by which time about half of the Guys and all of the Crossleys had entered service. (Birmingham City Transport)

Football Specials

1867

Parked in Garrison Lane, near the South Holme cul-de-sac, is Daimler CVG6 1867 (HOV 867). This was one of the stalwarts of Highgate Road garage which were always seemingly being used on the Inner Circle 8 route, where these workhorses seemed most at home. The Gardner 6LW 8.4 litre engine produced something of a snout-like bonnet and because they had less sound deadening material than the later 'New Look front' examples, always seemed to be noisy and have more vibration at high engine revs. Until 1948, St Andrews had been served by the Stechford tram routes, but for years afterwards the cobbled road surface remained in Garrison Lane, which really shook ordinary passengers, football supporters and bus crew about. (D. R. Harvey Collection)

A Demonstration Bus

3132

From time to time, manufacturers borrowed brand new buses prior to delivery to act as demonstrators for their product. From 15 December 1953 until 28 December 1953, BCT 3132 (MOF 132) was literally 'sent to Coventry' when Coventry Corporation was looking for an alternative engine to the AEC and Daimler engines fitted. The BCT Crossley-bodied Daimler CVG6, noticeably with its Birmingham municipal crests removed, pulls out of Broadgate on its last day of demonstration in Coventry on the 21 route to Alderman's Green. Behind it is a Coventry Corporation 83 (GKV 83), a Daimler CVA6 with a Metro-Cammell body which externally at least was based on the standard Birmingham design, which had a direct lineage to the Crossley body on 3132 in front of it. (T. J. Edgington)

Two Extremes of Birmingham Buses in 1953

Unidentified Guy at Metro-Cammell works

The 3003–3102 class of 27 feet 6 inch long Guy Arab IVs were constructed at the Elmdon works of Metro-Cammell. In 1947, Metro-Cammell had decided to make more space for railway carriage production by moving bus production from Washwood Heath to the former Austin Motors shadow aircraft factory at Elmdon which had assembled Short Stirling four-engined heavy bombers and flew them from the factory site using the adjacent Elmdon Aerodrome. One of these 1953 Guys stands outside the old hangers still with their war-time camouflage paint visible, in a semi-finished state. Except for the saloon sliding ventilators, the bus has been completely glazed. It lacks wings, but interestingly this view shows that while the body panels, as yet unpainted, are made of aluminium, the cab structure is made of steel. (D. R. Harvey Collection)

2608

On 30 January 1953, at about 4:40 on that Friday morning, 2608 (JOJ 608), a Guy Arab III Special with a Metro-Cammell H30/24R body, by then just 22 months old, left Acock's Green garage and took up duties as the first 44 from Acock's Green into the city. It never got there! At that time the early morning buses used Bradford Street in order to serve the early morning market workers and at the junction with Rea Street it was involved in an accident with a BRS lorry. The result was catastrophic as the bus hit virtually everything, including adjacent buildings and parked vehicles. Every side of the bus was severely damaged, with extensive frontal damage, severely damaged lower nearside body pillars, staircase and platform. Yet such was the strength of the Metro-Cammell metal-framed body that the bus was repaired and put back into service later in the year. (Birmingham City Transport)

Birmingham Trams 1953

1953 was the year that saw the end of tram operation in Birmingham, ending forty-nine years of faithful municipal service. There had been tentative plans to close the tram services in the city as early as 1944 but the need to make do and mend during the Second World War rather put an end to this and the final route closures were announced in 1948. Gradually the tram system was run down so that 1948 saw the closure of the Stechford routes, while in 1949 the Moseley Road group of routes and the Aston and Perry Barr services were abandoned. During 1950, the inter-suburban Lozells to Gravelly Hill route closed and, significantly, the tram routes to Washwood Heath and Alum Rock, which were the only ones in the city operated by bogie cars using bow collectors, also went. Originally these two services were due to be the last to be abandoned but in the event the air-brake cars were all transferred to Selly Oak depot, which along with Cotteridge depot, remained open until the closure of the Rednal and Rubery services along Bristol Road and the Pershore Road route on 5 July 1952. This did not get enough publicity as it was on the same day as the final closure of the London Transport tram system.

Throughout the rest of 1952, the 115 trams needed for the routes to Erdington, Short Heath and Pype Hayes were operated from Miller Street depot, though after 30 November thirty cars were stabled at Witton each night in order to allow for the gradual conversion of Miller Street for the replacement fleet of buses. By the end of June 1953 the number of operational trams had been whittled down to 104, with four trams in store in the works at Kyotts Lake Road, including trams 616 and 623, kept in reserve for virtually twelve months, having been earmarked to close the system.

This section of the book is divided up into clearly defined sections. Firstly there is a short look at the operating depots, followed by a journey out of the City Centre to Short Heath, Pype Hayes and Erdington during the first half of 1953, when normal tram services were operating. The third section shows the tour undertaken by cars 616 and 623 for the LRTL on Sunday 28 June 1953.

There is then a sequence of photographs taken on the last morning, including the passage of the last two ceremonial trams, again cars 623 and 616, to Erdington and the last service trams back to Miller Street and Witton depots. Finally, there is the movement across the city of trams making their way to Kyotts Lake Road for scrapping and the final sad scenes of trams being broken up at the Works.

In Service at the Depots

By 1953, there were only three places where Birmingham's trams could still be stabled.

Miller Street depot was opened on 4 February 1904 and was Birmingham Corporation Tramways' first tram depot, with capacity for twenty-four trams on five roads. Subsequent extensions enlarged depot to a capacity of 102 trams on seventeen roads. After the Bristol Road and Cotteridge route closures on 5 July 1952, it became the main operating depot for the Erdington group of tram routes. It was closed for trams on 7 July 1953 and was converted to a bus garage and was transferred to WMPTE on 1 October 1969. On the other side of Miller Street was the Permanent Way Yard, which was opened in December 1908 and had its own workshops and foundries. It was closed on 29 September 1952 and used for tram parking until closure for trams on 4 July 1953. It was then used to park buses from 5 June 1955. It was taken over by WMPTE in 1969 and is still in use by National Express for its training fleet and storing withdrawn buses.

Kyotts Lake Road was originally opened in February 1885 by the Birmingham Central Tramways as a steam tram depot and works. For a few years after 1904 the works built new tram bodies for both CBT and the Birmingham & Midland Tramways Company. It was transferred to BCT on 1 January 1907 with eight roads in the main works and five in the body shop. It ceased to be an operational depot in 1908, when it was totally converted into the main tram works. It was also used for trolleybus overhauls from 1925 to 1929 and from 1934 until the closure of the system in June 1951. It was closed in August 1953 after the last trams were broken up and sold in April 1954. It was used as industrial premises until part of it, that which fronted Kyotts Lake Road, was mysteriously burnt down in the early years of the twenty-first century.

Witton depot was built by Birmingham & Aston Tramways for its steam tram operation and was opened in 1882. Witton was converted to electric trams by City of Birmingham Tramways on 6 October 1904. It was taken over by BCT on 1 January 1912 with a capacity for fifty-eight trams on seven roads. It was closed as an operational depot after the closure of the Washwood Heath routes from 1 October 1950 but was retained for storage and scrapping. It was re-opened as an out-station to Miller Street in November 1952, closing on 4 July 1953 and used for scrapping trams and then to store new buses in the autumn of 1953 and the reserve pre-war bus fleet until August 1955. It was then sold to Dents, and later to Thomas Startin as a car showroom. After many years in the 1970s when it was empty, it re-opened in 1988 as Aston Manor Transport Museum and was used in this capacity until it was closed in unfortunate circumstances in 2011.

716, 674 (Above)
Miller Street depot had ten tracks leading directly off the street into some seventeen depot roads.
With a capacity, combined with the PW yard, reaching a maximum of 120 trams in January
1949, Miller Street was one of the largest tram depots on the system, being responsible for the 3
and 3X circular routes to Witton and the 6 to Perry Barr, which had been withdrawn by the end
of 1940, as well as the three Erdington routes and their respective shortworkings. Standing in the
entrances of the depot are a pair of Brush-bodied 40 hp trams, cars 716 and 674, while at the far
end is UEC-bodied 546 and car 637, the first of the MRCW trams. (D. R. Harvey Collection)

395 (Opposite, above)
Standing in Kyotts Lake Road with the tramcar works behind it on 29 June 1953 is car 395. Car 395
was selected to be preserved in November 1950, having been removed from the scrap merchant's
contract at a cost of £27 10s. 395, dating from 1912, was a UEC-bodied open balcony four-wheeler
and was one of the last surviving truck-mounted trams in the fleet. It was, however, not necessarily
typical of the BCT tram fleet, which since 1913 had been entirely made up of the much larger eight-
wheeled bogie cars. The tram was intended for static exhibition in the newly developed Birmingham
Museum of Science and Industry in the old Elkington's silver plating factory in Newhall Street. The
cost of its restoration was funded by the Cadbury's charity, The Common Good Trust. 395 was
taken in two halves to the new museum by 1 July 1953 and survives today at the Millennium Point
Museum in the Eastside development of the city centre. (D. R. Harvey Collection)

679 (Opposite, below)
Having just arrived at the entrance to Witton depot in March 1953 is Brush-bodied car 679.
The tram is about to be driven into the depot for overnight parking. On the last day of tramcar
operation on 4 July 1953, car 679 became the penultimate tram to operate on the 78 route
from Short Heath. With the stone plaque proclaiming BIRMINGHAM & ASTON MANOR
TRAMWAYS DEPOT, the depot, opened in December 1882, was built to house steam trams.
The City of Birmingham Tramways Company took over these routes on 30 June 1902 and
converted the Aston services to double-decker electric trams. After CBT closed, the depot was
transferred to Birmingham Corporation Tramways Department on 1 January 1912, when it held
thirty-eight trams on seven roads. The depot was closed on 30 September 1950 as an operational
unit, but after the depot had been used for breaking up the Bristol Road tramcars during July
and August 1952, Witton was used for overnight parking from 10 November 1952 for up to
thirty trams when conversion work at Miller Street began. (T. Barker)

549

During the conversion of Miller Street depot to buses, the Permanent Way yard, opposite the car sheds, was used to park trams in the open. This had previously occurred in the Second World War after the main depot had been bombed on the night of 9 April 1941, destroying sixteen trams. On Sunday 28 June 1953, on the occasion of the LRTL Tour of the Erdington routes by trams 616 and 623, UEC-bodied tram 549 stands just inside the entrance. As 549 was taken out of service just two days later, it is doubtful if it ever ran again in revenue service as it was taken to Kyotts Lake Road Works; yet this early removal to the scrapping lines meant that it was still extant on Tuesday 4 August 1953 as one of the last eight trams to survive. (A. N. H. Glover)

The Last Erdington Group of Routes

The final tram routes in Birmingham were operated to the north-east of the city, into the Erdington area, and from the abandonment of the Bristol Road group of routes on 5 July 1952, were for exactly one year the sole tram routes in the city. There were three routes, all of which left the city centre terminus in Steelhouse Lane and followed a common route by way of Aston Road, Aston Cross and Lichfield Road as far as Gravelly Hill. The three routes then split, with the straight-on line going to Erdington. This route was opened on 22 April 1907 and was eventually given the 2 route number. The Stockland Green tram service turned left at Gravelly Hill into Slade Road and was opened on 12 June 1912. This route was later numbered 1 and was extended to Short Heath along the reserved track in Streetly Road as the 2 route on 23 June 1926. The third tram route was along reserved track in Tyburn Road, initially as the 63 route which was opened on 13 May 1920 as far as Holly Lane. This service was extended to Pype Hayes Park as the 79 route on 20 February 1927. The final extension on the Birmingham system was that to Fort Dunlop in Holly Lane, which was opened on 12 February 1930. The last major alteration to the Birmingham tram system took place on 25 September 1938 when the 2 route was taken out of the narrow Erdington High Street and diverted on reserved track on the recently opened Sutton New Road by-pass. All these tram routes were closed on Saturday 4 July 1953.

547, 657, 679, 608 (Opposite, above)
On 22 June 1953, Miller Street still had 104 tramcars available for service, although over thirty trams were operated from the previously closed Witton depot while Miller Street was being converted into a bus garage. For the last year of tramway operation in the city, Miller Street had been the main depot for the remaining Erdington group of tram services. Although mechanical maintenance was done and trams were kept clean, there was a tired look to the condition of the trams as the time drew closer towards their final withdrawal. On Monday 22 June 1953, trams 547, 657, 679 and 608 stand at the entrance of the depot, representing four different classes of Birmingham bogie trams. 547 is a 37 hp tram built by UEC, originally with an open balcony, and was mounted on Mountain & Gibson bogies. 657 dated from 1923 and was built by MRCW, again originally with open balconies, on EMB Burnley bogies and was a 40 hp tram. 679 was constructed by Brush in 1924 while 608 was again a Brush-built tram with a 37 hp motor, but was originally open balconied and dated from 1921. However, to the normal passenger, they all looked exactly the same! (A. M. Wright)

City Centre

597
The conductor manhandles the trolleypole of car 597 as it stands at the 78 route barriers in Steelhouse Lane on 6 June 1953. Tram 597 had been used on the tour of the system on 23 July 1950, just before the closure of the Washwood Heath services on 1 October 1950, as it had just received an overhaul and repaint. 597 also had the distinction of being the last tramcar to be broken up at Kyotts Lake Road on 6 August 1953. Behind the tram is bus 2128 (JOJ 128), a 1951 Daimler CVD6 with a Metro-Cammell H30/4R body. The bus, which is working on the 29A route, is carrying the small Coronation flags just below the destination box. (D. Withams)

704, 645 (Opposite, below)
Travelling away from the Steelhouse Lane terminus, just past the Gaumont Cinema, on 17 May 1953 is Brush-bodied tram 704, which is working on the 79 service to Pype Hayes. Travelling inbound is MRCW-bodied car 645, which is working on the 63 route from Fort Dunlop. On the left outside the original Steelhouse Lane Police Station is a police-owned Austin A70 Hereford, a 2.2 litre four-cylinder car which although quite fast, with a top speed of just over 80 mph, was not very good at cornering at speed and was put in the shade by early Ford Zephyrs and of course the Jaguar Mark VII saloons. (R. Buckley)

556

Car 556 waits outside the Wesleyan & General Insurance offices at the Steelhouse Lane terminus of the 2 route to Erdington on Sunday 14 June 1953. This strengthened Brush-built tram of 1913 vintage is mounted on the standard Brush Burnley-type bogies and fitted with DK30/1L 63 hp motors. The leading driving wheels took up to 80 per cent of the total weight of the car, which gave excellent traction especially when accelerating and braking. The tram carries advertisements for Vernon's football pools and on the balcony dash one for W. M. Taylor, who were drapers based in Potters Hill, Aston. Car 556 saw service on the final day of BCT tram operation and was broken up at Witton in July 1953. (L. W. Perkins)

586

Entering Steelhouse Lane from Corporation Place on 28 June 1953 is car 586, the last of the 1914-built, UEC-bodied trams. Behind the tram is the General Hospital, dating from 1897, built in a handsome red-faced, terracotta-faced brick to the designs of William Hennan, and just in front of the tram are two Midland Red buses, the leading one being a one-year-old Brush-bodied BMMO D5B, which is being followed by an-EHA-registered SOS FEDD. Tram 586 was fitted with EMB Burnley bogies and re-motored with Dick, Kerr DK30B 40 hp motors from damaged trams during 1943, and had its body strengthened in December 1949. This tram was one of ten of the 512 class to be fitted with the eight-windowed top decks in 1929, when it was also fitted with enclosed balconies. (A. D. Packer)

694

Leaving Steelhouse Lane and the General Hospital behind, 40 hp Brush-bodied totally-enclosed sixty-three-seat car 694, dating from January 1925, is working on the 79 service to Pype Hayes in May 1953. It was the last tram to work on the 63 shortworking and was the last tram to use the cross-over at Kingsbury Road in Tyburn Road on the final morning of operation. After leaving service, car 694 went to Witton depot for scrapping. (R. Grosvenor)

556, 662
In May 1953, cars 556 and 662 pass each other in Corporation Place. Brush-bodied 40 hp tram 662 is travelling on an outbound 2 route to Erdington while UEC-bodied tram 556 is working into the nearby Steelhouse Lane terminus on the 78 route. Both trams would operate on the last day and were transferred to Witton depot, where they would be broken up. Towering above the Austin K4 lorry is the imposing General Hospital, while the building behind the Triumph Mayflower is the King Edward Buildings, designed in 1900 at the northern end of the somewhat curtailed development of Corporation Street. For many years the ground floor was dominated by one of John Hawkins' drapery shops. (R. Grosvenor)

559, 700
As the trams descended Steelhouse Lane, they passed the General Hospital, outside which is bus 2737 (JOJ 737), a 1951 Daimler CVD6 which is picking up passengers going to Kingstanding on the 33 route. On 22 June 1953, car 559, one of the UEC-bodied trams dating from 1914, originally with open balconies, works on the 78 service to Short Heath and follows Brush-bodied car 700, which is ten years newer. Car 700, working on the 2 route to Erdington, is crossing the junction with Loveday Street as it is about to pass the impressive Crown Buildings and enter the distant Corporation Place. (D. R. Harvey Collection)

549, 729

Dominating Corporation Place since 1935 has been the Central Fire Station, with its large clock tower over the main central yard entrance, although fire engines left through the large red doors in Corporation Street. Passing through the middle of the traffic island towards Aston Street on the right on 25 May 1953 is car 549, a 63 hp UEC-bodied tram working on the 2 route to Erdington, while 729, one of the thirty 40 hp Brush-bodied trams delivered in 1925, travels into the city centre, also on the 2 route. Cars 549 and 558 were the only trams to operate on the last day of the Bristol Road group of services on 5 July 1952 and on the final day of the Erdington routes on 4 July 1953. The traffic island had been built when the old Georgian buildings on the site of the new fire station were demolished, although the Nechells trolleybuses had to go around the island. (L. W. Perkins)

Aston Road to Gravelly Hill

581
Travelling into the city on Aston Road on 2 July 1953 when working on the 2 route from Erdington is UEC-bodied tram 581. When this tramcar was new, it was briefly used in February 1914 as one of the four First Class trams used on the which had been opened during the previous September Hagley Road service. This tram was rebuilt in 1943 using EMB Burnley bogies and English Electric 40 hp DK30B, reclaimed from damaged trams. The tram has just crossed the bridge over the Birmingham & Fazeley Canal and is about to pass the factory of Powell Brothers, who were tube manufacturers. 581 would be in the last batch of trams to travel across the city centre via Carrs Lane and Moor Street to Kyotts Lake Road Works on the evening of 4 July 1953 for scrapping. (T. Barker)

717
The Thursday prior to the final closure was 2 July 1953 and a normal tram service was being operated without a hint of the events of the next two days. Cars 717 and 728 are both travelling into the city along Aston Road when working on the 2 route from Erdington. They are passing Aston Brook Street on their nearside, while opposite them the wires just visible on the left lead into Miller Street and thence onto the depot. Between the two city-bound trams is the exposed gable wall of the printers Whitehouse & Co. and the low advertising hoardings which marked the culverted location of Aston Brook. Coming out of Miller Street is a Fordson 7V van, while the car at the rear of the queue of traffic is a 1937 Lancaster-registered Austin Cambridge. (A. D. Packer)

645, 713
The Coronation of Queen Elizabeth II had taken place just four days earlier on Tuesday 2 June 1953 when MRCW car 645 and Brush-built tram 713 both lead long lines of inbound and outbound trams along Lichfield Road at the Aston Cross tram station. Towering above the tramcars is the imposing Ansells Brewery, which was still decorated with the Coronation slogan of 'LOYAL GREETINGS FROM THE HOME OF ANSELLS'. On the left of the brewery is Park Road, which led up the hill and then down, passing Aston Hall, Aston Parish Church and then on to the terminus at Witton Square. This was the 3X route, which was closed on New Year's Eve 1949, leaving behind the ghostly remains of the tarmac-covered tram tracks. (L. W. Perkins)

645, 639 (Opposite, below)
Parked at the tram railings alongside the entrance to the subterranean gentlemen's lavatory at Aston Cross is tram 645, working on the 2 route to Erdington. In front of the tram is a 1946 Ford E83A 5 cwt van. On the far side is Park Road is the early Victorian row of three-storied buildings which included Wimbush's, the Small Heath-based baker, and Thompson's, the pork butchers. Following 645 is car 639, which is being used on a 78 service to Short Heath. Both these DK 30B 40hp trams belonged to the class of twenty-five sixty-three-seat cars built in 1923 which spent their entire lives at Miller Street depot. The order was placed for the bodies with the Washwood Heath-based Midland RC&W, who had rarely built electric double-deck tramcars. The company claimed that they could deliver the entire batch in sixteen weeks, which Mr A. C. Baker, the Birmingham General Manager, doubted was possible. BCT offered to lengthen the terms of the contract, but by the time sixteen weeks had passed, not one of the tramcar bodies had been completed. BCT invoked the 'period for completion' clause in the contract, resulting in the reduction of the company profits to virtually nothing and the dismissal of one of the MRCW management. Despite their somewhat unfortunate start to life, the 'Midland' trams all remained in service until mid-1952, giving excellent service and achieving a maximum of 941,000 miles in service. (C. Carter)

721, 542

The Aston Cross junction had tram-loading barriers which were used by all the Lichfield Road routes. This busy intersection had also been served by the 3X tram to Witton, which was abandoned on the last day of 1949; that route had followed the line of the buildings behind the clock tower. Car 721 is just manoeuvring over the crossover and its trolley-pole is already on the out-of-city wire; this in turn is delaying car 542, on its way to Erdington on the 2 route. This all took place on the last evening of tram car operation, when the Victorian shopping centre, dominated by the wonderful smells coming from the HP Sauce factory and Ansells Brewery, was still thriving and before urban renewal began to cater for cars rather than people, leaving the area as a large traffic island and very little else. (T. J. Edgington)

548

Approaching Aston Station Railway Bridge on an inbound 78 service on 1 July 1953 is UEC-bodied tramcar 548. The tram is passing the office of the Continental Express Company, while a customer is standing on the step of Ted Hitchman's butchers shop. On the nearside of the tram is an overloaded pre-war Bedford lorry which appears to be carrying sacks of vegetables. On leaving the compulsory tram stop on the right, the overhead wiring was arranged so as to pull the tram's trolleypole to the nearside and level with the roof of the tram. There were only two other low bridges on the system, that at Dudley Port, which ceased to be used in 1939, and that at Selly Oak Station over Bristol Road, whose tram services had recently been abandoned on 5 July 1952, and all had wiring that was similarly lowered. (A. Yates)

684

Once beyond Aston Hall Road, Lichfield Road passed Salford Park and the junction with Cuckoo Road, where the tramway occupied a short 600-yard length of reserved track. Here 684, one of the Brush-bodied 40 hp cars, is working along Salford Bridge Road on an outbound 2 service to Erdington. Tram 684 was one of 354 bogie cars in Birmingham, all of which had maximum traction bogies; these 'all-electric' trams were built with Dick, Kerr DK 40 hp motors and EMB Burnley units with outer 31¾ inch driving wheels. In the background is the King Edward VII public house, which dated from 1904 and was demolished in 2011; it was located on the corner of Lichfield Road and Aston Hall Road. (R. Grosvenor)

662 (Opposite, above)

The former LNWR railway bridge across Lichfield Road at Aston was rebuilt on Sunday 25 March 1906 to accommodate, initially, CBT's open-top electric double-deck cars. Although the road was subsequently lowered, it was always a tight squeeze to get a standard 15 feet 6 inch top-covered tram beneath the bridge. The 1-20 Class, the 71-220 Class and most of the ex-CBT top-covered cars were prevented from passing beneath Aston bridge because they were too tall. Brush totally-enclosed car 662, the first of the class of twenty constructed in 1924, is about to pass beneath it on its way from Pype Hayes on Monday 25 May 1953. Car 662 would remain in service until the last day of tram operation but would go to Witton depot for scrapping rather than to Kyotts Lake Road Works. To provide sufficient clearance, the overhead wires were at the side of the road so that the trams' trolley-poles were level with the car roof. On the extreme right, on the corner of Holborn Hill, is the splendid Victorian Britannia public house, dating from 1898. Holborn Hill led to Aston Motive Power depot, which was numbered 3D and was one of the main locomotive sheds in the Birmingham area. (L. W. Perkins)

691

Crossing Salford Bridge, opened in 1926 to carry Lichfield Road over the Birmingham & Fazeley Canal and the River Tame, is Brush-bodied car 691, which after assembly at Hockley depot had entered service in January 1925. This sixty-three-seater was mounted on EMB maximum traction bogies and was powered by two DK30B 40 hp motors. These trams, which were built to the standard BCT length of 33 feet 6 inches, spent their entire lives operating from Miller Street depot. The tram is working on an inbound 79 service from Pype Hayes and is being followed over the bridge by a mid-1930s Standard Ten. 691 would operate on the last day and was driven from its last service duty directly to Witton depot for breaking up. (S. Eades)

617

37 hp motored Brush-bodied car 617, built in 1921, is working the 5.15-mile-long 79 route from Pype Hayes towards the city and is standing at the impressive Gravelly Hill tram shelters on 24 May 1953. The tram has just turned from the wires to the right in Tyburn Road. Car 617 had been briefly placed in store at Kyotts Lake Road Works as one of nine trams held in reserve and re-emerged during September 1952 to resume operations at Miller Street depot. It is extolling the delights of the locally made Typhoo Tea on the main side-panel advertisement. (J. C. Gillham)

Short Heath 78 Route

646

Turning out of Slade Road into Gravelly Hill is car 646, working into the City on a 78 route. The trams took 52 minutes to do the round trip from Steelhouse Lane to Short Heath, but after buses replaced them, the journey time was reduced by ten minutes. Built in 1923, 646 was one of the twenty-five MRCW-bodied trams which were the first in the Birmingham fleet to have totally-enclosed balconies from new. On 4 July 1953, the last day of operation, 646 was operating on the same 78 route to Short Heath and was terminated at the Victoria Road junction on the inbound service before being taken directly to Witton depot where, before the end of the month, it would become one of the forty-four trams to be broken up there. Unrecognisable today, this part of Gravelly Hill is hidden by Junction 6 of the M6 motorway, better known as Spaghetti Junction. Dominating the area then was the Erdington Arms public house, which was an Atkinson's Brewery hostelry. (D. R. Harvey Collection)

637

Climbing Copeley Hill in Slade Road on Monday 4 May 1953 is car 637. The tram is on an inbound 78 service and is passing the side of the Erdington Arms public house as it approaches Gravelly Hill. Looking in remarkably good condition, the tram is passing a Birmingham-registered Morris Eight dating from 1937. This tram was the first of the 1923 MRCW tramcars and had a pair of DK30B 40 hp motors driving a pair of EMB Burnley bogies. This type of maximum traction bogie had the large 31¾ inch wheels at the outer end and these took about 80 per cent of the car's weight and provided sufficient downward force on the rails to enable smooth acceleration and deceleration without slipping. The trailing pony wheels on each bogie were 21¾ inches in diameter and enabled the tram to be both longer than a four-wheeled tram and provide stability when negotiating a curve. (C. C. Thornburn)

658

The former LNWR Aston and Lichfield railway line passed over Slade Road by means of an attractively porticoed skewed bridge, underneath which tramcar 658 is about to pass on its way to Short Heath on the 78 route. It is May 1953 and the tram car is speeding towards the first row of shops in Slade Road and the just visible Victorian gable ends of Slade Road Junior and Infants School. The railway line marked a noticeable delineation of urban land use, with an Edwardian suburb beyond the bridge towards Stockland Green, while behind the tram and back to Gravelly Hill it was more industrial. Two trams could pass each other under the bridge but they took up virtually all of the road space; pedestrians were given the added luxury of their own footpath on one side of the road. (H. Brearley)

645 (Opposite, below)

Waiting at the Streetly Road terminus of the 78 Short Heath service is MRCW car 645. The driver of the tram stands on the step and watches for his departure time to come round on the Bundy Clock. He will then 'peg the clock' with his key and then set off down the steep hill on the reserved track towards Stockland Green, Gravelly Hill and Aston Cross to the city terminus in Steelhouse Lane. The extension from Stockland Green to Short Heath was opened on 23 June 1926, making the third from last route extension on the BCT network. This was in order to cater for the large municipal housing estate, whose houses are seen in the background, in Short Heath Road. (D. R. Harvey Collection)

721

This view of Stockland Green, looking towards the city on a rainy day in April 1953, reveals the distant Slade Road, lined with Edwardian and late Victorian houses. From here, Slade Road descends in a continual drop for about one mile to just beyond the railway bridge near to Gravelly Hill. Car 721, one of the GEC WT32H 40 hp-motored, Brush-built trams of 1925, stands at the original 1912 Stockland Green terminus, loading up with some rather damp-looking passengers when working on a 78 going to the city. The 702-731 class were the last 'all-electric' trams bought by BCT as after this batch was delivered, all future purchases were equipped with air brakes. On the left is The Snack Bar, where the tram crews would leave their billycans to be collected on their next journey so they could get a hot cup of tea. (A. M. Wright)

586

Car 586 stands at the terminus of the Short Heath route in Streetly Road in May 1953. This tram was one of ten of the 512 class to be fitted with the eight-windowed top decks in 1929, when it was also fitted with enclosed balconies. This design of top deck had been first introduced on the air-brake 762 class Brush-bodied trams, introduced with bow collectors in 1928 for use on the Washwood Heath services. All the 1920s extensions of the tram routes which were built on reserved tracks had large, green-painted wooden tram shelters and here, at Short Heath, there was one such impressive structure. Some of these survived the abandonment of their associated tram routes and were used by the replacement bus services. (R. Grosvenor)

698, 722 (Opposite, above)

Leaving Gravelly Hill, Tyburn Road led towards Fort Dunlop and Pype Hayes. The road was built during the First World War as a joint venture by the Corporation and the Dunlop Rubber Company but was only opened to trams on 20 February 1920. By 1953, the road was served by the 79 route to Pype Hayes and the short working 63 service into Holly Lane which terminated in front of Fort Dunlop. Car 698 is turning into Tyburn Road on an outbound 79 service, while approaching Gravelly Hill on an inbound 79 service is car 722. Both trams had Brush bodies although electrically they were different as 698 had a Dick, Kerr DK30B 40 hp motors while 722 had GEC WT32H 40 hp motors. Cars 698 and 722 were in service on 4 July 1953, 698 operating on the same 79 service. (D. R. Harvey Collection)

Pype Hayes 79 Route

722
Leaving Wheelwright Road and the distant Navigation Inn behind, car 722 speeds along the reserved track, passing the Concentric Manufacturing Company factory on its left, outside which is an early post-war Atkinson six-wheel flatbed lorry. The tram, a Brush bodied sixty-three-seater with GEC WT32H 40 hp motors is working on a city-bound 79 service on Monday 4 May 1953. Travelling in the opposite direction is a Hillman Minx Phase III. 722 was one of the last batch of twenty-four trams to be moved across the City to Kyotts Lake Road Works via Carrs Lane to Moor Street for scrapping on the evening of 4 July 1953. (C. C. Thornburn)

670

Just about to pull away from the tram shelter in Tyburn Road in June 1953 is car 670. The tram is working towards Pype Hayes on a 79 service and is in the cut-through of the traffic island in Tyburn Road at the junction with Bromford Lane. This is where the Outer Circle 11 bus route crossed Tyburn Road, one of whose bus shelters is visible next to the disappearing motorcyclist. To the right of the tram is the Navigation Inn, a large 1920s suburban public house. This 40 hp Brush-bodied EMB Burnley bogie car dated from 1924 and is carrying advertisements for CWS and Save, and on the balcony panel one for Bovril, both of which were typical of advertisements carried by Birmingham trams in their last few years. (G. Burrows)

587

The Fort Dunlop siding was opened on 13 February 1930, at the expense of the Dunlop Company, when suitably decorated ex-CBT tram, car 472, which in theory could never have worked the whole route as its height precluded it from passing beneath Aston Station railway bridge, was used to cut the ceremonial tape. It was an impressive layout in Holly Lane, with kerbside loading set against a background of playing fields and a crown green bowling green and factory reminiscent of the Cadbury factory at Bournville. The impressive Fort Dunlop proclaims the name of the Belfast veterinarian who invented the pneumatic tyre in 1888, although he was bought out by other entrepreneurs, such as E. T. Hooley, as early as 1895. By 1915 a 260-acre site had been chosen in open countryside in the Tame Valley and Fort Dunlop was quickly constructed in order to be operational and provide materiels for the Great War effort. Car 587 stands at the tram shelters in Holly Lane on 22 June 1953. This tram was the first of the fifty Brush-built sixty-two-seaters which when new had open balconies, the last trams delivered to the Corporation with this feature. Equipped with Brush Burnley bogies and the rather slow BTH GE 249A 37 hp motors, which were replaced between 1927 and 1929 by 63 hp DK30/1L motors, car 587 was one of only nine of the class to have its body strengthened, resulting in the elimination of the bulkhead windows on the platforms. Behind the tram is bus 1330 (FON 630), a 1942 'unfrozen' Leyland-bodied Leyland Titan TD7 which is working on the 40 route to Lozells, which until 1950 had been the 5 tram route, Birmingham's only inter-suburban tram route. (A. N. H. Glover)

562, 548 (Opposite, below)

The very last tram extension to be built in Birmingham was that from Tyburn Road along Holly Lane to the Fort Dunlop factory on the south side of the Birmingham & Fazeley Canal bridge. Holly Lane was a private road belonging to the Dunlop Company. In May 1953 car 562 is crossing the junction with Holly Lane on a city-bound 79 service while similar tram 548, surrounded by workers leaving the Dunlop factory on their bicycles, waits to turn out of Holly Lane on a 63 service. Both trams were built in 1913 and had UEC bodies, originally with open balconies, which were enclosed in the mid-1920s. Mounted on M & G Burnley bogies, both trams were re-motored again in the 1920s, with a pair of BTH GE249A 37 hp motors which gave them a sedate rather than sparkling performance. Trams 548 and 562 were taken out of service on Friday 3 July 1953 and were broken up at Kyotts Lake Road Works. (T. Barker)

640

MRCW-bodied tram 640 of 1923 is approaching the terminus at Pype Hayes on the 79 route in May 1953. The central reservation by this time was looking a little overgrown as the abandonment was imminent. The Birmingham Corporation Housing Department's council housing was developed throughout the outer suburbs of the city in the interwar period, the Pype Hayes development containing 1,344 houses. This placed it only twelfth out of fifteen major housing schemes built between the wars in the city. Some of these houses are on the right-hand side of Tyburn Road. Car 640 would remain in service until taken to Kyotts Lake Road Works on the evening of Friday 3 July for breaking up. W. T. Bird of Stratford-upon-Avon was given the task of breaking up all the trams after 1950, which it did with ruthless efficiency. (A. N. H. Glover)

573

By 1953, the state of the track on the remaining reserved tracks, especially along Tyburn Road and Streetly Road, was beginning to deteriorate as it was not worth repairing or replacing unless it had become dangerous. This had been the case on the reserved track on Bristol Road South when, due to the state of the tracks, two trams passing at speed had swayed into each other. In Tyburn Road, alongside the outbound tram which is approaching the Pype Hayes terminus, the inbound tracks look distinctly out of alignment. UEC-bodied car 573 had DK 30/1B 40 hp motors and was on EMB Burnley bogies for its last ten years of service and was one of the last eight trams to move along the streets of the city when it was moved from Miller Street depot to Witton depot on the evening of Tuesday 7 July 1953. (C. Carter)

640

Despite all the contractual problems with their construction and delivery, the MRCW cars proved to be a very sound investment for BCT, and only six of the 637-661 class failed to see service over the last few days of operation. Car 640 is standing just short of the end of the tracks on Sunday 17 May 1953, having just arrived from the city centre. Just in front of the tram across Chester Road was the huge Bagot Arms public house, opened in November 1931, and the large, 111-acre Pype Hayes Park, opened in 1920, when Tyburn Road itself had been opened. The park was sufficiently large that it was something of a recreational focus for the north side of the city. Additionally, a 108-acre, 18-hole golf course was on the north side of Plants Brook beyond the park. (A. N. H. Glover)

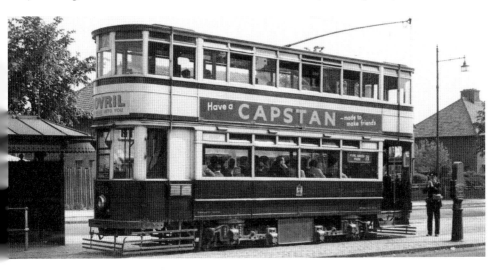

622

Standing alongside the distinctive wooden shelters erected at the end of the reserved track at the Pype Hayes terminus in Tyburn Road is a somewhat rebuilt Brush-bodied tram 622. This tram was one of three of the class that were fitted with an eight-windowed top deck in the style of the 1928 762 class of trams. 622 received this top deck in July 1928, while it was additionally strengthened in 1949, receiving steel plating which eliminated the lower saloon bulkhead window and the first lower saloon ventilators next to the platforms. These trams had Brush Burnley bogies, and once re-motored with 63 hp DK30/1L motors were the fastest trams in the fleet for the last year of the system. (L. W. Perkins)

Erdington 2 Route

716

Leaving the Six Ways, Erdington, Junction, the 2 route passed along Gravelly Hill North, lined with large late nineteenth-century villas in their own grounds. The route then dropped down to the wide open spaces of Salford Bridge and then into the industrial area with Victorian terraced housing in the Aston area. Car 716 had just completed its last revenue service on the 2 route and, at 7.30 p.m. on 3 July 1953, is returning to Miller Street depot. After the final closure on the folowing morning, 716 was kept in Miller Street but as scrapping began at Witton depot and space was made, this was one of eight trams transferred from Miller Street to Witton between 7.15 p.m. and 8.15 p.m. on the evening of 7 July, making this one of the last tams to run on the streets of Birmingham. (D. R. Harvey Collection)

690

Destined to be the last service tram on the 2 route to Erdington, leaving Steelhouse Lane at 10.42 a.m., car 690 travels along Sutton New Road beneath rather sagging overhead. This bypass route was introduced on 25 September 1938 and allowed for the 2 route and its shortworking, the 64 to Barnabas Road, to work along the central reservation. It is Sunday 28 June 1953 and car 690 saunters along the almost deserted carriageway on its way to Erdington. It is passing Barnabas Road on the left with the NHS local 'clinic' while opposite is the Erdington Branch Post Office. Car 690 had a Brush-body and Dick, Kerr DK30B 40 hp motors. (A. D. Packer)

566 (Opposite, above)

On 2 July 1953, car 566 has just descended Gravelly Hill when working on the 2 route into the city. It had passed the Erdington Arms public house on the corner of Slade Road as it enters the tram station at Gravelly Hill. 566 had been re-motored in 1927 with English Electric DK30/1L 63 hp motors and, after the abandonment on 5 July 1952 of the Bristol Road and Cotteridge routes, was one of just eighteen 'all-electric' trams to have this more powerful set of motors, which gave it a much better performance than the rest of the surviving fleet, which only had 40 hp motors. To the left of the tram is a Vulcan 6PF lorry, which is being followed across Gravelly Hill by a Vauxhall Wyvern LIX. (D. R. Harvey Collection)

704

Descending the narrow section of Sutton Road from Erdington is Brush-bodied car 704, which is approaching the tram stop outside the yard of the Erdington Jig & Tool Company during June 1953. The prospective passengers are already walking into the roadway as the tram approaches, something that would be considered highly dangerous, nay impossible, in twenty-first-century traffic conditions. It is close to the junction with High Street and Station Street. Briefly capturing the feel of the hamlet that once was Erdington, the tiled-roof cottages and shops bear testimony to years of neglect. The tram is passing St Thomas and St Edmund Roman Catholic Church, built in the Decorated style in 1848 to the design of Charles Hansom. The entrance to the churchyard is seen behind the trees on the left. (D. R. Harvey Collection)

696 (Opposite, above)

On Wednesday 10 June 1953, Brush-bodied tram 696 leaves the Chester Road traffic island as it travels towards the city when working on the 2 route. This must have been a warm evening as all the upper saloon windows are wide open. Following the tram is a Ford Anglia E93A with an almost unburstable 933cc side valve engine. The rebuilt wartime Midland Red bus is working on the hourly service to Mere Green on the 103 route and has just passed the bus stop on the left attached to the traction pole. Alongside the bus on the next traction pole is a square ALL TRAMS STOP HERE sign. Car 696 would remain in service until 3 July, when it was taken for Kyotts Lake Road Works for breaking up. (D. R. Harvey Collection)

677

The third traffic roundabout through which tramcars passed on the Erdington route was at the Sutton Road/Chester Road junction. Here, just beyond the Yenton public house, car 677, one of the usual 40 hp Brush cars of the 662 class, has just left the terminus and the driver is looking out for traffic on the island before accelerating across Chester Road. The Edwardian shopping area around the road junction was always considered to be a somewhat superior part of north Birmingham: 'A dormitory borough of considerable charm with a cross section of all social groups in the population, but an unusually large percentage of well-to-do business and professional people.' Sutton Road continued beyond the city boundary into the even more select Sutton Coldfield. Although Sutton had plans for a tram service, it never materialised and Midland Red took over the option on the route, although double-decker buses were not allowed into Sutton until 1938. This was because it was thought by the local residents that they might intrude into the privacy of large residential buildings along the route. (A. W. V. Mace)

632

As the driver of the tram walks to the front of Brush-bodied car 632, having just 'pegged the Bundy Clock', his conductor walks back to the rear platform of his tram ready to start collecting the fares after the tram has left the Erdington terminus. By this time, somewhat perversely, all the Miller Street-operated routes were the first to be completely converted to 'Ultimate' ticket machine operation, replacing the old Bell Punch system. The new bus stop for the impending replacement buses, behind the Ford Consul EOTA, on the corner of Broadfields Road, is already in place. The Ford is only a few months old as it had been registered in Birmingham in March 1953. (D. Caton)

581

The terminus of the Erdington service was on a short length of side reserved track in Sutton Road, some two hundred yards beyond the traffic island at the Chester Road junction. Car 693 has to wait for the tram at the terminus to leave before it goes into the single-line stub beside the distant shelves of the driver and conductor of the other tram; the crew of car 693 has a considerable wait ahead of them. Few Birmingham bogie cars carried advertisements until after the Second World War, and when they did it tended to spoil their appearance. Car 581, a Brush-bodied car which had entered service some forty-nine years earlier in 1914 as an open balconied, vestibuled tram, has a number of dented panels and looks a little 'battle worn' as it waits at the terminus on 22 June 1953. The tram crew pose for the photographer as they wait to return to Steelhouse Lane, some 5 miles away. Standing next to the driver on the platform is the well-known Birmingham-born transport photographer Norman Glover, who many years later became a dear friend of the author. (A. N. H. Glover)

573 (Opposite, below)

On 7 June 1953, UEC-bodied car 573 stands in the lay-by at the terminus of the 2 route in Erdington. This was virtually at the city boundary and just visible through the trees alongside Sutton Road is the Sutton Coldfield boundary sign. The track here was a single spur which led up to the passenger shelter, but usually, especially in off-peak periods, the trams would be stopped at the Bundy Clock, as is the case here, in order for the driver to peg the clock more easily. Many of the Edwardian-built shop frontages still have the bunting from the Coronation some five days earlier. (J. H. Meredith)

The Events of Sunday 28 June 1953

The LRTL organised a tour of the remnants of the Birmingham system on Sunday 28 June. The first stage of the tour would go to Witton depot by way of Aston Cross and Park Road before returning by way of Victoria Road, then going to each of the three surviving termini in turn at Short Heath, Erdington and Pype Hayes as well as the branch to Fort Dunlop in Holly Lane. The two tramcars returned the party back to Miller Street depot before returning to the Steelhouse Lane terminus. 616 and 623 then returned empty to Kyotts Lake Works.

616
Loading up with members of the Light Rail Transport League and their invited guests in Steelhouse Lane outside the Wesleyan General Insurance Company offices just before 3 p.m. on Sunday 28 June 1953 is car 616. Behind it is similar tram 623, both of which had been cleaned and polished for this, the last ever tour of the Birmingham tramway system. The next time they would be used was as the official trams for the closure of the system. (D. R. Harvey Collection)

623 (Opposite, above)
Standing in the entrance of Gate 1 at Witton depot on 28 June 1953 is the second of the LRTL tour tramcars. 623 is in front of car 616, which is parked inside the depot. Above the group of LRTL members are some of the service cars, though during the time that Witton was used for overnight storage from November 1952 as an overflow for Miller Street, trams were not operated out of this depot on Sundays. On Tuesday 7 July, three days after the final tram abandonment, car 623 was to become the last passenger tram to run on the streets of Birmingham. It was moved from Miller Street back here to Witton, arriving there around 8.15 p.m. Despite being in good condition, having had a second 'spit and polish' clean prior to its use as the penultimate car in the closing ceremony, the powers that be did not stand on ceremony as the Birds scrap men broke up the car by 14 July 1953. (J. S. Webb)

616

About to leave Witton depot in Witton Lane and facing Villa Park is car 616. The Co-operative shop in the background is in Witton Square, through which the Outer Circle 11 bus service passed. Above car 616 is the comparatively new roof of Witton depot, which was only put on the tram depot in 1946 after the direct hit by a bomb on 4 December 1940 which destroyed the existing roof, bringing it down on the trams stabled inside and resulting in the loss of fifteen tramcars. Brush-bodied tram 616 is about to leave and travel to Short Heath by way of Victoria Road, Lichfield Road and Salford Bridge. (A. N. H. Glover)

616, 623
Standing alongside each other in Park Road on 28 June at the cross-over are the two LRTL tour trams, car 616 on the left and 623 on the right. The trams have left Witton depot and have climbed the hill, passing the magnificent Jacobean Aston Hall on their right, and have stopped at the junction with Victoria Road. Here the trams will both negotiate the point work in order to turn to the left into Victoria Road and thence on to Lichfield Road. The complicated manoeuvre had to be done in this manner as there was only a single track turning into Victoria Road. (D. R. Harvey Collection)

616
Parked in the terminal siding in Erdington is car 616, which is being used on the LRTL tour. Behind it is normal service car 717, which is working on the 2 route, though the crew and the passengers must have been a little irritated being boxed in by the pair of crowded tour tramcars. The tram tour carried some 142 tram enthusiasts on this final trip around the Birmingham system. Car 717 was one of thirty 'all-electric' tramcars built in 1925 by Brush with GEC WT32H 40 hp motors and which also worked in service on the last morning of services. (D. R. Harvey Collection)

623 (Opposite, below)
Having arrived at the Short Heath terminus in Streetly Road in front of car 616, this was the first of many opportunities for the tram enthusiasts to get off the two trams in order to take photographs. Both trams were built in 1921 and were bodied by Brush with open balconies, which were enclosed during the late 1920s, and had a seating capacity of thirty-four in the upper saloon and twenty-eight in the lower. They were fitted after 1927 with DK30/1L 63 hp motors, which replaced the original GE 249A 37 hp motors. All of this class numbered 587-636 were mounted on Brush Burnley bogies. 623 was one of nine of the class to have its body strengthened, revealed by the plated-over platform window alongside the entrance steps. (A. Yates)

623

The last terminus to be visited on the LRTL Tour was that at Pype Hayes. The 79 tram route was extended from Holly Lane to Pype Hayes Park, just short of Chester Road, on 20 February 1927 and although the city boundary was over half a mile away at Hanson's Bridge Road, the crossing of Chester Road was perceived as something of an obstacle and so this was as far as the trams ever got. Ironically, the replacement 66 bus route went as far as the boundary and had a special turning loop in the throat of Hanson's Bridge Road. Amid the sward of milling tram enthusiasts, car 623 stands nearest the end of the tracks in Tyburn Road while car 616 faces the city. In this view, the two cars reveal that they both carried the SAY CWS AND SAVE advertisements on the panels between the decks. (A. N. H. Glover)

566, 597, 691, 623, 658 (Opposite, above)

The interior of Miller Street in the weeks before the conversion to buses was somewhat untidy as rails were being lifted, pits were being filled in and the new flooring for the buses laid down, all while the trams were still operating. To alleviate the congestion, some thirty of the 104 trams were stabled overnight at Witton and a number of trams were parked in the Permanent Way yard on the opposite side of Miller Street to the depot. On 28 June 1953, the last Sunday before the final closure, from right to left, cars 566, 597, 691, 623 and 658 stand in the depot amid all the builders' rubble. Car 623, the LRTL tour tram, has been parked inside the depot while 616 is actually standing outside in Miller Street. Tram 597 would have the unenviable distinction of being the last tram to be cut up at Kyotts Lake Road Works just five weeks later on Thursday 6 August 1953. (A. D. Packer)

668

The parking of about eight trams in the Permanent Way yard in Miller Street was a tight squeeze, with three trams fitting on the single track in front of the office block on the left and the remainder parked in 'line astern' facing the exit to the yard. Brush car 668, carrying the advertisement 'SAY CWS AND SAVE' on the side panel between the decks has been shunted forward on to the 'office block' line. This 40 hp Brush-bodied sixty-three-seater mounted on EMB Burnley bogies had been allocated to Miller Street depot since it entered service in 1924 and would operate for the last time on the day before the abandonment on Friday 3 July. (A. N. H. Glover)

616

The well presented car 616 is well loaded with tram enthusiasts as it turns at the Miller Street junction in Aston Road, with Hubert Street and its bay windowed terraced Victorian housing to the left of the tramcar. To the right of the tram is the row of three-storied nineteenth-century buildings with a row of shops including the premises of Brookes Opticians, a company that had six branches around Birmingham's suburbs. Behind the tram is the inspector, who was using a point changer in order to manoeuvre the tram across the points. (J. Eades)

623 (Opposite, above)

After the LRTL tour of the last parts of the tram system ended in Steelhouse Lane, cars 616 and 623 were driven back to Kyotts Lake Road Works, where they would be prepared for the closing ceremony on the following Saturday. Car 623 passes through the middle of the traffic island at Camp Hill with the Ship Hotel, also known as Prince Rupert's Headquarters 1643, dominating the junction. In this condition, it does seem a pity that this tram was not saved for preservation. The saloon car overtaking the tram is an Austin 16, the largest of the early post-war Longbridge products, with a powerful 2,199cc four cylinder engine. (T. J. Edgington)

616

Waiting to reverse from Stratford Road, in Sparkbrook, into Kyotts Lake Road is car 616 with 623 behind it. The two trams have completed their penultimate duty by being the vehicles used by the LRTL to tour the Erdington routes some six days before the closure of the system. Prior to the abandonment of the Stratford and Warwick Road tram services on 5 January 1937, the tram tracks disappeared beyond the distant buses to both Hall Green, at the city boundary with Shirley, and Acocks Green. The tracks in this part of Sparkbrook were retained in order for the trams to gain access to the works. The bus working on the 24 route from Warstock is 2846 (JOJ 846), a Daimler CVG6 with a Crossley H30/25R body which had recently entered service in November 1952. This bus was destined to have a very long life, as it was one of the last of what latterly became known as 'Birmingham Standards' to be withdrawn at the end of October 1977. (A. N. H. Glover)

616

The two tour trams were parked inside Kyotts Lake Road on the evening of 28 June 1953, in company with car 655. This tram had been in the works since May, having been selected as the best car to be used as a spare. It even received new dash panels but was never returned to service again. Works car PW8, cut down from an open-top ex-CBT tram, 505, in December 1920, was kept for shunting tramcars around the works prior to breaking up and indeed PW8 was the last tram to be driven on the road in Birmingham when it moved under its own power into Kyotts Lake Road on 6 August 1953 prior to being despatched on one of Bird's lorries for scrapping at Stratford. On the far side of the works is car 710, while in the foreground is a preserved EMB Burnley-type bogie from car 638 which would later become an exhibit along with preserved tram 395 at the Museum of Science and Industry in Newhall Street. (A. N. H. Glover)

710

Along with a few stored Daimler COG5 buses, 1197 (FOF 197) and 1210 (FOF 210), car 710 stands against the wall inside the Works on 28 June 1953. This tram had been withdrawn with flat wheels in June 1953. Amazingly, it was used as a test for the 'decorated' final tram, car 616, when the wording THE END was daubed on the dash panels and BIRMINGHAM'S LAST TRAM along both sides. It was all rather shabby, but as the offer by P. W. Lawson, the Superintendent of the Kyotts Lake Road Repair Works, to have an illuminated final car had been rejected by the Transport Committee, this is the best they could do at the Works to make a valedictory statement about the passing of Birmingham's trams. The thousands of staff who had worked so proudly keeping the Corporation tramcars in immaculate condition would have been either very embarrassed or turning in their graves at this miserable send-off to the tramcars which had served Birmingham for just over forty-nine years. (A. N. H. Glover)

The Last Day, Saturday 4 July 1953

The closing ceremony for the Birmingham tram system was a slightly tawdry affair. The Transport Department wanted to have a low key ending and the opportunity to have a final illuminated tram was turned down. Car 616 looked as though someone had scribbled on it the inscriptions BIRMINGHAM'S LAST TRAM and THE END, yet a withdrawn tram had been practiced on to get this scruffy effect. Birmingham deserved better!

Several abortive attempts to preserve one of the 'all electric' bogie cars based at Miller Street were turned down, leaving the UEC-bodied four-wheeler 395 to be preserved as the sole surviving Birmingham tramcar. So despite cars 616 and especially the penultimate tram 623 being immaculately maintained and kept at Kyotts Lake Road Works, having led sheltered non-operating lives since the closure of the Bristol Road group of services exactly one year earlier, both trams were used for the closing ceremony and then quickly despatched for scrapping.

546
Surrounded by crowds trying to catch either one of the last trams or just trying to catch a glimpse of one of the last trams before they disappeared from the streets of Birmingham forever, UEC-bodied tramcar 546 waits outside the Wesleyan General Building in Steelhouse Lane. This tram was one of twenty-eight of the class re-equipped with 63 hp DK30/1L motors in 1927 and had its body strengthened in 1948, thus eliminating the platform bulkhead windows. On the last morning there were still sixty-four trams available for service, though not all of them were required. Car 546 was one of two extra tramcars drafted in to provide 'Extras' for those wanting a last tram ride on the 2 route; the other tram involved in this was 679. (D. R. Harvey Collection)

690

The last tram in passenger service was Brush-bodied 40 hp car 690, which left the Steelhouse Lane terminus at 10.42 a.m. on the 2 route to Erdington. Just visible chalked on the waistrail is the inscription 'IT'S BEEN A GOOD UN'. It is passing the General Hospital in Steelhouse Lane which was opened in 1897, having been designed by William Hennan, on the site of a Georgian hospital originally opened in 1779. Leaning from the upper balconies are some of the hospital staff, who on this Saturday morning are watching a significant historical event. Only a few minutes later, the next vehicle to Erdington on the replacement 64 route was bus 2301 (JOJ 301), an exposed radiator Crossley-bodied Crossley DD42/6. Tram 690, also watched by quite a number of interested people in Steelhouse Lane, is about to cross the junction with Loveday Street, just beyond where the Standard Vanguard is parked, and go towards Corporation Place. (R. Knibbs)

578

Having left Steelhouse Lane at 10.37 a.m., by the time 690 had departed as the last tram to Erdington, car 578 was at Aston Cross being met by a large crowd of well-wishers. Again suitably inscribed in chalk, with 'THE LAST ONE TO S HEATH' on the waistrail and 'WELL DONE OLD TIMER' on the dash, this tram was indeed the last one to Streetly Road, Short Heath. On its inward journey, the tram transferred its passengers in Lichfield Road at Victoria Road, but unlike most of these transfers it ran back to Miller Street, where it remained until later the same evening before joining the last convoy of twenty-four trams across the city to Kyotts Lake Road Works. (C. Carter)

620 (Opposite, above)

Moving across the points in Sutton New Road at the Barnabas Road cross-over is car 620. This Brush-bodied 63 hp tram was originally built with open balconies and seating for sixty-two passengers but in the late 1920 the balconies were enclosed and the previous staggered seating in the upper saloon was replaced by a more normal in-line layout which increased the overall seating capacity by one to sixty-three, with the seats being upholstered rather than the original wooden 'park bench' type. The tram is displaying the correct 64 route in the side destination box for this outward journey, but the end number box has been turned to show 60, used for shortworkings to Aston Cross. Car 620 never made that junction as it was stopped short at Victoria Road, where its passengers were transferred to a waiting bus, and the tram was driven directly to Witton depot for scrapping. (A. N. H. Glover)

560

In Tyburn Road car 560 approaches the terminus located opposite the Bagot public house, having left Steelhouse Lane at about 9.55 a.m. To the right of the tram, through the trees, is the small bell tower of St Mary's Anglican church on the corner of Padstow Road. This church was completed in 1930 to the design of E. F. Reynolds at about the same time as the Corporation's council housing, which lined Tyburn Road, was built. A brand new tram replacement MOF-registered Guy Arab IV waits at the tram terminus for the last passenger cars to Pype Hayes to arrive from the city when 608 was the penultimate tram and 569 was the final tramcar on the 79 route. Tram 560 was taken to Kyotts Lake Road for scrapping later the same evening. (J. Eades)

556
One of the trams which did run to Witton depot after it had finished its last passenger carrying duties was car 556, again one of the long-lived 63 hp UEC-bodied bogie cars dating from 1913, which had had its body strengthened in 1948. It is travelling back towards Aston on one of the last 78 services from Short Heath and is passing Salford Park, adjacent to the nineteenth-century Salford Bridge Reservoir. The tram is about to enter the short stretch of reserved track in Salford Bridge Road. There was a distinct lack of observers of the passing of the trams on this part of the route, save for the owner of the motorcycle combination. (A. N. H. Glover)

713
Having worked on one of the last trams from Erdington on 4 July, 40 hp Brush-bodied bogie car 713 had its passengers transferred to the waiting buses, in this case one of the new buses working on the replacement 64 bus service. Once empty, the trams travelled a little way up Lichfield Road and turned right into Victoria Road. From here it was a one way trip to Witton depot for breaking up. (A. Yates)

646 (Opposite, below)
At 10.50 a.m., MRCW-bodied tram 646 stands in Lichfield Road having returned on one of the last 79 tram services from Pype Hayes. The trams stopped here and the passengers were transferred to a waiting bus which had the appropriate new route number display. In this case, the bus is 3015 (MOF 15), a brand new Guy Arab IV with a Metro-Cammell H30/25R body which had only been licensed four days earlier. This bus would later become one of the last ex-Birmingham 'Standards' to remain in service, not being withdrawn until the end of October 1977. The tram has written, somewhat poignantly, in chalk on the dash panel 'GONE HOME' and 'MY LAST FAREWELL'. Overtaking the tram is Midland Red double-decker 2568 (HHA 20), a 1944-vintage Guy Arab II with a Weymann body much rebuilt by Brush just two years earlier, which would only add another four years to the life of the bus. 646 would be driven directly from here along Victoria Road and Park Road before reaching Witton Lane and entering Witton depot for the last time. (R. Knibbs)

674

On the very last day of tramway operation, Saturday 4 July 1953, the Lichfield Road trams ran normally until mid-morning, when they operated from the outer termini to Victoria Road. City-bound passengers were then transferred to buses and the cars then ran either to Witton depot via Victoria Road or to Miller Street. It really is a case of 'ring out the old, ring in the new' as passing on the replacement 66 route is a brand new bus, 3026 (MOF 26), a Guy Arab IV with a Metro-Cammell body. Brush-bodied tram 674 is in Aston Road North, at the junction with Miller Street, where it would be driven for parking until it was transferred to the Works later the same evening. (A. N. H. Glover)

573, 578

UEC-bodied cars 573 and 578, both dating from 1914, stand forlornly in Miller Street depot at 12.20 p.m. on 4 July 1953 after they had both run into the depot after operating on this, the last Saturday morning of the passenger service. 578 had been the last tram to Short Heath just about two hours earlier. Car 578 was moved to Kyotts Lake Works that same evening. Car 573 had not been used on the last day but was one of eight trams moved to Witton on the evening of 7 July 1953 for scrapping. The enthusiasts are making their final farewells to the trams, which still retained an air of shabby dignity. (A. N. H. Glover)

569 (Opposite, below)

The last tram on the 79 route to Pype Hayes was car 569, which had left Steelhouse Lane at 10.35 a.m. The tram returned to Lichfield Road, where its passengers were transferred to a waiting bus. Having completed its last run, as shown by the chalked inscription 'THE LAST 79' on the waist panel, this UEC-bodied tram is being watched by a crowd in Aston Road as it turns into Miller Street as it went back to the depot. Car 569 had been rebuilt in 1943 with EMB Burnley bogies, English Electric DK 30B 40 hp motors and replacement controllers salvaged from stored war-damaged trams. (A. N. H. Glover)

The Final Closing Ceremony

The final closing ceremony used two tramcars. The penultimate tram was the highly polished 623, which carried retired tramway employees and was driven by Ernie Worrall, who had joined the Transport Department in 1915, and conducted by Arthur Birt. The last tram was car 616, carrying the Lord Mayor and Lady Mayoress, the General Manager Mr W. H. Smith and senior members of the Transport Department. This tram was driven by Frank Bissell, who had driven the same tram on the previous weekend's LRTL tour, and whose service with the Department began in 1914, and conductor Henry Bond, who actually collected *6d* fares from the guests! This section takes a generalised view of this trip and therefore only shows the progress of these trams to Erdington and back.

The iconic photographs of the final tramcar procession on 4 July were taken from the upper storey balustrade of the Wesleyan General Building in Steelhouse Lane. The very large throng of people who had come to say a fond farewell to the last Birmingham trams was really quite amazing, spilling over the pavements and blocking the roadway. Car 616, unsuitably decorated with the words 'THE END' at either end of the platform panels, stands at the loading barriers just before its departure time of 10.48 a.m. At this moment it is displaying the correct 2 route number but this was soon altered to show 1 to signify the last ever tram. (L. W. Perkins)

623

The two ceremonial trams and their invited passengers left Miller Street depot at 10.18 p.m. and waited for ten minutes for the last service trams, car 690 being the last, to travel into the city to the Steelhouse Lane terminus. Car 623, with 616 just visible behind, stands at the bottom of Miller Street at the Aston Road junction just a few minutes after leaving the depot, watched by a number of well-wishers who have come to bid their farewells to the trams. (A. Yates)

616

The last tram, car 616, travels through the traffic island in front of the Central Fire station on its way through Corporation Place to Steelhouse Lane, having come from Miller Street depot. By this time the large number of people lining the route had held up the tram, so that by this time 616 was about ten minutes behind schedule. The tram drivers had each been presented with a bouquet by the residents of Miller Street and one of these had been tied to the fender of car 616. (R. Knibbs)

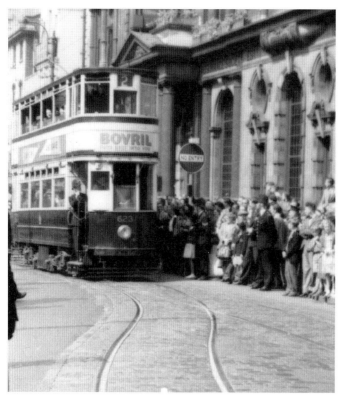

623
There was a very large crowd blocking the area around the tram terminus in Steelhouse Lane outside the Wesleyan & General Assurance Building as the last two trams prepared to go on their ceremonial last run to Erdington. The two trams had changed places, with car 623 standing in front of 616. It left the terminus about a minute before the last painted-up tram and retraced its steps down Steelhouse Lane to Corporation Place.
(D. R. Harvey Collection)

616
With the Wesleyan & General Assurance clock showing 10.48 a.m., Birmingham's last tram, decorated car 616, is about to leave the terminus in Steelhouse Lane on the 2 route to Erdington. Passengers on the top deck have pulled the saloon windows right down and are waving enthusiastically to the hundreds of people who had turned out to watch the final journey of the last official tram procession. (B.C.R.L)

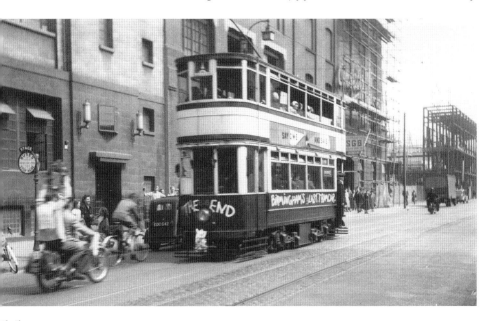

616

Passing the new bus stage for the 66 route to Eachelhurst Road, car 616 is passing the large Ansells Brewery building just beyond Aston Cross in Lichfield Road and picks up speed as it follows car 623, which is just out of sight. The tram still has its bouquet of flowers on the rear fender. By now a motley collection of motorbikes, cyclists and old cars was following the final tram procession, many of them being owned by students. (R. Grosvenor)

623

The penultimate tram, car 623, crosses the points at the Victoria Road junction, which is blocked by people who came out to say goodbye to the trams. In the distance, the decorated tram, 616, is catching up. The crowds have impeded the progress of this procession, causing 623 to travel at a crawl. During the morning, some thirty-four trams, having completed their last passenger-carrying journeys, turned right off Lichfield Road and into Victoria Road on their way to Witton depot for scrapping. (D. R. Harvey Collection)

616

Passing the Victoria Road junction in Lichfield Road is the decorated tram 616, moving slowly through the crowds towards Aston Railway Station. In the distance, alongside a Midland Red SOS FEDD, is car 623. Just visible is one of the last service trams, unloading its passengers, who are being transferred to one of Miller Street depot's exposed radiator Crossleys. Parked in Sandy Lane, on the right, is one of the new MOF-registered Guy Arab IVs fitted with Metro-Cammell H30/25R body, which is waiting to move around the block and pick up further exchange passengers from the trams terminating in Lichfield Road. (A. Yates)

616

By the time Brush-bodied decorated car 616 had reached Salford Bridge, it was 11.05 a.m. and the last tram convoy was already some fifteen minutes late. This was due to its slow progress through the crowds of people wanting to see Birmingham's last tram and the surrounding convoy of bicycles and cars. The tram is approaching the Salford Bridge tram station. In front of the tram is a much rebuilt Austin Seven which was somewhat overloaded with students, one of whom had a trumpet and who frequently played 'The Last Post'. (R. Knibbs)

616, 623

Parked in Sutton Road just short of Chester Road, with the large Yenton public house in the background, are the two last trams which were used in the closing ceremony on 4 July 1953. Just beyond the pub, on the opposite side of the road, was the terminus of the Erdington tram service. With crowds gathering outside Thomas Lackenby's restaurant and Morril's ladies hairdressers' premises, both tramcars are posed alongside each other. The top deck destination boxes show different 'route' numbers; although the trams were working on the 2 route and displayed ERDINGTON 2 in the side boxes, car 623 showed the number 2, denoting that it was the penultimate tram, while car 616 showed 1 as it was the last tram. (J. Eades)

616

The crows were still out in force in Miller Street by the time the final tram procession returned from Erdington at about 11.58 a.m. Car 616 proceeds slowly into Miller Street depot for the last time. Obsessively wanting to get rid of the trams as quickly as possible and not to encourage souvenir hunters, car 616 was transferred to Witton depot later the same evening, with car 670 coming back to Miller Street to make room for the last tram. The end came quickly for 616 as despite its virtually overhauled condition, it was broken up inside an hour on the morning of 7 July 1953. It was, if not actually THE END, symbolically one of the more significant events after the closure of the Birmingham system. At least one of the platform panels with THE END painted on them was presented to the General Manager, Bill Smith, and apparently still survives today. (D. R. Harvey Collection)

Trams Going To Witton and the Convoys to 'The Lake'

At the end of passenger services on the morning of 4 July, trams coming into the city were taken out of service in Lichfield Road and were then driven directly to Witton depot by way of Victoria Road, Park Road and Witton Lane. That morning, thirty-four trams made this one-way journey. Over the last two evenings, something more spectacular happened which involved the majority of the BCT tram fleet. Mention has been made of the last movements of Birmingham's tramcars in convoys travelling across the city from the Miller Street depot to Kyotts Lake Road Works in Sparkbrook for breaking up on the evenings of 3 and 4 July. This is an amalgam of those journeys taking the cars from Dale End to Kyotts Lake Road on this, the tramcars' last, one-way trip. The journey across the city was complicated because the police would not allow the trams to go down the still-wired Albert Street against the flow of the one-way traffic. As a result, the trams had to gain Moor Street from High Street by way of coasting down the hill on which Carrs Lane stood as the overhead wiring had been removed earlier in the year.

To Witton

662

Thirty-four trams were sent directly out of service from Lichfield Road to Witton depot for storage and swift breaking up. Car 662, the first of the Brush cars from the 662-701 class, had entered service in March 1924 and spent the whole of its working life at Miller Street depot. This tram was in store from December 1941 as it required major repairs, at first at its home depot, though latterly it was at Washwood Heath depot until it was returned to service during October 1945. On 4 July 1953 car 662 was travelling down Park Road, Witton, on its way to its final period of storage prior to being broken up later the same month. (A. Yates)

713
Turning in front of the impressive St Peter and St Paul Parish Church in Witton Lane is Brush-bodied 40 hp car 713, making its way on its final journey to Witton depot on 4 July 1953. This tram had been transferred to Witton in December 1940 to replenish that depot's bomb damaged stock when nine of the class were destroyed on the night of 4 December. It had been a Miller Street car, but by transferring it to Witton, car 713 missed the bombing of Miller Street on the night of 9 April 1941 when a total of twenty-four trams were totally destroyed. This is where the next car in the class, car 714, overturned on 14 March 1940, injuring thirty passengers and destroying itself. The original Aston Parish Church was noted in the Domesday Book and in the middle of the wall of the south aisle there is a little fourteenth-century stonework remaining. The 144-feet-tall steeple dates from the fifteenth century, although it was partially rebuilt in 1777. Otherwise the church dates from a design by J. A. Chatwin and was rebuilt between 1879 and 1890. (D. R. Harvey Collection)

620

Passing Villa Park, 'The Theatre of Dreams', the home of Aston Villa FC, car 620 travels along Witton Lane, kicking up the dust in the tram tracks as it is driven to the distant Witton depot. Brush bodied tram 620, which had 'NOW 66 BUS' chalked on the dash panel, had only been in service less than half an hour earlier and still had its 79 destination number displayed in the top balcony box. This was unusual, as even after the trams had come out of service for the last time, as conductors were professional to the last, they tended to wind the blinds to 'DEPOT ONLY'. This thirty-two year-old tram was within minutes of being parked up for the last time. The advertisement on the corrugated iron gable end of the Witton Lane stand is for Herculs bicycles, which were made in Rocky Lane, Aston. (D. R. Harvey Collection)

692

Parked in Witton Lane alongside the advertisement hoardings at the Witton end of Villa Park is Brush-bodied bogie car 692. This tram had earlier worked on the 2 route to Erdington, hence the chalked inscription '64 BUS' and 'TA TA'. In the distance, outside the Aston Hotel, which dates from 1910, another tram reverses into Witton depot for the last time. In a few minutes 692 would travel to where the crowds of people are standing opposite Witton depot watching the trams going into the depot for the last time. It was an incident outside the Aston Hotel that lead to the murder in November 1923 of Tommy Ball, a young Aston Villa centre half, by an off-duty policeman. (B.C.R.L)

Miller Street to Kyotts Lake Road

686, 665

It is the evening of Friday 3 July 1953; thirty-four trams, withdrawn that day and not required on the final morning's services, were driven from Miller Street depot via the city centre to Kyotts Lake Road Works for scrapping. The trams queued up in Dale End outside the Cine Equipment shop that sold movie projectors. Brush-bodied tram 686 has just started to accelerate across the Albert Street junction and get into High Street. (A. N. H. Glover)

583

UEC-bodied tram 583 had entered High Street and its trolleypole is already pulled down as it begins to coast around the corner into Carrs Lane, where gravity will take it down the 150-yard-long hill and around the corner into Moor Street, where it would be able to pick up power again. This curious spectacle was watched by inquisitive passers-by, checked by Transport Department Inspectors and observed by the police. Behind the tram, coming out of Albert Street, is a bus on the 37 route to Hall Green, worked by a 1949-vintage HOV-registered Daimler CVG6 with a Metro-Cammell body. (T. J. Edgington)

Service Vehicle 15
Not wishing to leave anything to chance, parked outside the Oxford Restaurant and Snack Bar (whose
meat pies were gorgeous!) on 3 July 1953 was Service Vehicle 15 on its usual 925 OP Trade Plates.
This was BCT's mobile crane, but it was not parked at this spot for use in that capacity. It had been
specially fitted with a stout bumper across the radiator so that if a tram got stuck anywhere on the
unwired section of track, it would be used to shunt the car for the rest of its thwarted progress. It seems
strange that this steel bar was fitted in order that the trams could be given a push without denting
their platform panels as the trams were going for scrap anyway! Perhaps this was the last throw of the
tram mens pride in their doomed fleet? Over the next two days, such was the skill of the tram drivers
that the vehicle was only required once. This breakdown vehicle had been built as a demonstrator
for Birmingham Corporation in 1931 as one of only three six-wheel AEC Renown 663s not built
for London General, the other two going to Glasgow and Northampton Corporations. Fitted with
a Brush H33/25R body, it was registered MV 489 and given the fleet number 92. It was only in
service until 1937, when it was converted into this magnificent beast. Nicknamed 'The Ambulance', it
survived until 1961 in the BCT service fleet. (G. F. Douglas, courtesy A. D. Packer)

678 (Opposite, below)
Freewheeling down Moor Street on the evening of 4 July is another of the 40 hp Brush-bodied
totally-enclosed bogie trams dating from April 1924. This was to become one of the last trams to
be broken up during 4 August 1953. On the rear platform is one of the many enthusiasts, who
is holding the trolleypole rope and will put it back on the overhead once around the corner in
Moor Street. With present day Health & Safety legislation, this action would be unimaginable,
though in 1953 it was almost welcomed by the Transport Department staff. (J. C. Gillham)

698

On the evening of 4 July, having been used in the morning on the Short Heath route, car 698 is coasting around the curve from High Street into Carrs Lane. In attendance, as usual, is the AEC Renown service vehicle, waiting to be of use as a shunter if a tram stopped on the unwired section. In the background, in High Street, is the temporary Henrys Department store building, built on a wartime bomb site on the corner of Martineau Street which had served until 1950 as the city terminus of the Washwood Heath routes. (J. C. Gillham)

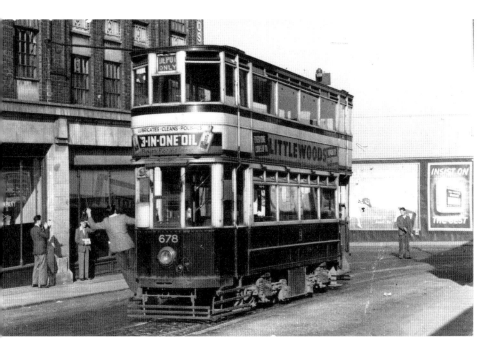

586

Car 586, with its eight-window top-deck, suffered the indignity of being the only tramcar to fail to coast all the way down the hill in Carrs Lane and into Moor Street. It had not managed to gain enough momentum in High Street before the pole was pulled down and so became the only one of thirty-six trams to require assistance. The tram is being gently pushed by the AEC Renown breakdown lorry in front of The Corner public house, to where the overhead wires were still in situ on the Friday evening, 3 July. (G. F. Douglas, courtesy A. D. Packer)

674

Once into Moor Street, the trams proceeded on the inbound tracks before using the cross-over on the road over the railway tunnel between Moor Street Station and Snow Hill Station to gain the outbound tracks. Car 674, another one of the 662-701 class of 40 hp trams dating from 1924, had just made this turn and is moving towards this cross-over with the trolleypole reversed. In the background is the large, white F. W. Woolworth store in the Bull Ring, in front of which the tram will turn left as it goes on its last journey to the waiting scrap men at Kyotts Lake Road Works. (J. C. Gillham)

656
Turning out of Moor Street into the Bull Ring at 6.50 p.m. on the evening of 3 July is MRCW 40 hp bogie tram 656. The tram was being driven to Kyotts Lake Road Works for scrapping. In the background, partially hidden by the trees, is St Martin's Parish Church, a restrained building in a fourteenth-century Gothic style which was completed in 1875. In front of the church are the black and white-painted bus shelters used exclusively by Midland Red for their service to the south of Birmingham. (R. Grosvenor)

548
UEC-bodied 63 hp car 548 takes the curve from Moor Street into the Bull Ring for the last time on 3 July 1953. Behind the tram stands the Market Hall, built in 1834 with a Doric entrance façade and said to be the finest market hall in England. This and the early nineteenth-century shops higher up the Bull Ring towards New Street were all swept away in the 1960s Bull Ring development scheme. In front of the Oswald Bailey shop on the corner of Moor Street is a Standard Vanguard Phase 1 saloon. The overhead above the tramcar has a double wire hanger, a remnant of the Coventry Road trolleybuses, which were abandoned on 30 June 1951. (D. R. Harvey Collection)

665

Once the trams had descended the Bull Ring on their way to the works in Sparkbrook for scrapping, they entered Digbeth, one of the original parts of medieval Birmingham which stood at a crossing point of the River Rea's flood plain. Brush-bodied car 665 turns into Rea Street from Digbeth in front of the impressive Digbeth Civic Hall, which had been officially opened on 16 January 1908 with a main auditorium seating 2,000. The exterior is a mixture of red brick and grey terracotta forming the more ornate features of the façade including the three towers. On the left, next to the Belisha Beacon, is the edge of the open air site at the front of Midland Red's bus garage which was used to park buses. (G. F. Douglas, courtesy A. D. Packer)

557

Bradford Street was originally the main drovers' route from the south of Birmingham into the markets in medieval times. Yet it took the nineteenth century industrial development to put an end to this routeway's primary function. Climbing the deserted Bradford Street at 7 p.m. while being transferred from Miller Street to Kyotts Lake Road Works for scrapping on the evening of 4 July 1953 is UEC-bodied tram 557, which was one of twenty-eight of the 512-586 class to be re-motored in 1927 with 63 hp GEC DK30/1L motors. A lone Warwickshire registered Austin Cambridge 10/4 dating from 1938 stands almost at the corner of Alcester Street, opposite the Miller Works of Alfred Bird, the well-known custard manufacturer. This tram was still intact on 1 August but was broken up that day. (A. N. H. Glover)

597 (Opposite, below)

At the other end of this short section of Rea Street, the trams turned left into Bradford Street. Car 597, looking very smart, having just been repainted, had been used on 19 July 1950 for that year's LRTL tour, which included a last visit to the Alum Rock 8 and Washwood Heath 10 routes as well as the interurban 5 route from Lozells to Fort Dunlop. This 63 hp Brush-bodied tramcar built in 1920, with its body strengthened in 1948, takes the turn as it proceeds to Kyotts Lake Road Works on 3 July 1953 as one of thirty-seven trams which were moved from Miller Street depot. (G. F. Douglas, courtesy A. D. Packer)

546, 722
Passing through Camp Hill on the evening of 4 July 1953 are two trams on their way to Kyotts Lake Road Works for breaking up. In the distance, near Camp Hill Railway Bridge and kicking up the dirt in the tram tracks, is Brush-bodied car 722. The tram going through the centre of the traffic island is UEC-bodied 63 hp bogie car 546. This tram had been used in the morning to provide an 'extra' on the 2 route along with car 679. On the left, about to negotiate the island in front of The Ship Hotel, is 2065 (JOJ 65), one of Yardley Wood garage's Daimler CVD6s with Metro-Cammell bodies which would be working on either 13A or 24 routes. (G. F. Douglas, courtesy A. D. Packer)

679
Having worked as an extra on the 2 route on the Saturday morning, Brush-bodied car 679 had, later that same evening, the dubious distinction of being the last tram to enter Kyotts Lake Road Works prior to being broken up. This was one of a number of tramcars that had inscriptions chalked on their dash panels, in this case 'GOOD BYE BRUM' and 'THE END'. Disproving the old adage 'last one in, first one out', 679 was one of twenty-four trams that were more or less still intact on 1 August and was not dismantled until 5 August. It is turning from Stratford Road into Kyotts Lake Road alongside the Black Horse, an Atkinson's Brewery-owned public house. (G. F. Douglas, courtesy A. D. Packer)

627

Turning into the main entrance of Kyotts Lake Road Works on 3 July 1953 for the last time is Brush-bodied car 627. It would be another month before this tram would succumb to the scrap men's torches. On the Friday evening there were only a few people watching this first convoy to the Works. The line-up of parked cars is interesting as they are all Corporation-owned Austin A40 four-door Devons, while in front of it is one of Barford Street garage's Daimler CVG6s, 1890 (HOV 890), waiting as a transfer vehicle to take the tram crews back to Miller Street after their last ever tram driving duty. (A. N. H. Glover)

726, 705, 578

On 4 July 1953, having arrived in Kyotts Lake Road Works, the trams came in through the single-line entrance and on to the traverser in the foreground in the main repair shed. The traverser then took each tram sideways across the works onto the next available track space; the tram was then driven into the parking space and the procedure then continued until the works was full up. Parked behind the traverser, looking ready to go back into service, are cars 726, 705 and 578, all of which would be broken up before the end of the month. (L. W. Perkins)

Breaking up the Trams

Witton had been almost exclusively where Birmingham's trams had been broken up since the closure of the Washwood Heath routes in October 1950. Over the next three months at the end of 1950, sixty-five trams were dismantled at this depot, including the last twenty-nine four-wheel trams, these being the last of the 301-400 class. In the early part of 1952 another eight bogie cars were broken up at Witton. After the closure of the Bristol Road and Cotteridge routes on 5 July 1952, all the 70 hp trams and all surviving air-brake trams, i.e. all trams numbered between 732 and 843, were broken up here, with 130 trams being dismantled in July and August 1952. After the final abandonment, a total of forty-four trams were broken up by W. T. Bird at Witton depot during July 1953, which was done very much 'behind closed doors'.

Meanwhile, at Kyotts Lake Road Works sixty-five trams were broken up, with the last tram being dismantled on 6 August 1953. Access to Kyotts Lake was much easier and as a result there were far more opportunities to photograph the death throes of Birmingham's tram fleet.

646
At the end of July 1953, very few trams were left in Witton depot. On the right are the lower saloons of a pair of bogie trams, while over the pits on the left are three trams, of which MRCW tram 646 is the only one that is identifiable. It is surprisingly complete, even retaining its window glass, which was usually taken out at the earliest opportunity. Witton depot was subsequently used to store new buses and some pre-war buses kept in reserve for about eighteen months after the last of the trams had gone. (D. R. Harvey Collection)

560, 546

With a background of Victorian terraces in Grafton Road, car 560, with 546 behind, waits the attentions of the cutters' torches in the yard of Kyotts Lake Road Works in front of the paint shop on 24 July 1953. Surprisingly, this building and the huge wooden doors still survive at the time of writing, some sixty years after they last saw a tramcar. Behind car 546 was Brush-bodied tram 632 but all three had been broken up before the end of the month. As was normal procedure, the fleet numbers and legal lettering had been painted out. Sixty-five cars were broken up at these premises after the final Erdington abandonments and this process took nearly five weeks. (A. N. H. Glover)

726, 608, 578

Standing in the repair shed of Kyotts Lake Works on 24 July 1953 are cars 726 (on the left), 608 and 578. The two trams on the left had bodies built by Brush and are indistinguishable from each other, while the UEC body on 578 was slightly different, with the balcony window below the route number destination box being square, as opposed to the others, whose similar windows were rectangular. The window glass on all these trams had been removed and the first and last body pillars in the upper saloon had been cut in preparation for the top-deck to be lifted off the rest of the tram. (A. N. H. Glover)

PW8
Destined to be the last car to run under its own power, PW8 still has the unenviable job of shunting redundant trams in the former repair shed at Kyotts Lake Road Works on 28 July 1953. A number of trams, glassless and pillarless, stand forlornly with the oxy-acetylene bottles poised for the next session of the scrapping operation. The blackboard to the right shows the final locations of individual trams in the eight roads of the works. In the foreground is the traverse which ran the width of the repair shed and served all the eight tracks. (A. N. H. Glover)

633
The remnants of Brush-bodied tram 633 stand in Kyotts Lake Road Works on 28 July 1953. With its staircase going upwards to nowhere, the top deck has already been put on one of Bird's low-loaders. The platforms have been cut from the rest of the lower saloon and hang rather sadly off the remains of the tram. On the right is car 632, and on the far right car 572, which are both surprisingly intacrt, though soon they would both be reduced to the same state as 633! (A. N. H. Glover)

597

The scrapman's oxy-acetylene cutting torch is working overtime as the last passenger tram to be broken up, Brush-bodied car 597, still fairly complete, begins to succumb to its final dismantling on 6 August 1953. The pillars in the top deck have been separated from the lower saloon. It was a sad end to not just this tram but to the whole fleet, which was consigned to bits with inglorious haste. Alongside 597 is works car PW 8, which had been used throughout the scrapping process at Kyotts Lake Road Works to shunt the double-deckers into position for breaking. (L. W. Perkins)

597

As had occurred with all the trams that were broken up at 'The Lake', the top-deck was cut away from the lower saloon and hoisted by a mobile crane onto an articulated trailer which had been reversed into the main entrance. On 6 August the top-deck of car 597 had been removed and was being hoisted off the lower saloon prior to being placed on the waiting trailer. One of the mechanics is already beginning to remove the leading bogie prior to both bogies being placed inside the lower saloon body. (L. W. Perkins)

597

Only a few hours after work had begun on its dismantling, the remains of the lower saloon of car 597 sits on the somewhat battered articulated trailer owned by Birds of Stratford which is parked in Kyotts Lake Road. The lower saloon was used rather like the hull of a boat, with the pair of bogies dumped where once the upholstered seats were. One of the staircases reaches upwards to its missing upper deck, which by this time was already on its way along the A34 to Birds' scrapyard in Stratford. All the trams scrapped by Birds suffered this sad, ignominious end. (A. N. H. Glover)

PW8

This really was THE END. In the early afternoon of Thursday 6 August 1953 shunter PW8 made the last move of a Birmingham tram under power when it was driven out into Kyotts Lake Road for a final group photo of the remaining staff at 'The Lake'. Watched by a small crowd of former employees, P. W. Lawson, the depot superintendent, chalked 'The Lot' on the water tank, while other chalked tributes read THIS IS THE END, FAREWELL TO BIRMINGHAM and SHE'S BEEN A GOOD-UN. There was no standing on ceremony as within a few minutes it was on a low-loader going to Bird's scrapyard in Stratford. (A. N. H. Glover)

PW 8

PW 8 was the last tram to run under its own power in Birmingham after it was used as the works shunter. It was driven out of the Works into Kyotts Lake Road on 6 August 1953 and after it was photographed it was winched onto the articulated low-loader behind W. T. Birds' AEC Matador. It would then take its final journey to Stratford. It was therefore unique in that it was the only scrapped car to leave 'The Lake' complete, all the others leaving in pieces. A bid was made for PW8 by Llandudno & Colwyn Bay Tramway Company but it apparently came too late as the tram had reached Birds' quarry off Birmingham Road, Stratford-upon-Avon. This, just as car 616 had predicted a month earlier, really was 'The End'. (A. N. H. Glover)

PW8

With barely anyone left to watch its final departure, PW 8 is carried on the low-loader down Kyotts Lake Road. The ex-RAF AEC Matador towing wagon is about to turn left into Stratford Road, but has to wait for the traffic, including an almost brand new Midland Red LD8, one of the 100 Leyland-bodied Leyland Titan PD2/12s, to pass. The bus, ironically, could be working on the 150 service to Stratford, the destination of the former CBT tram which had been converted from open-top tram 505 in December 1920. (A. N. H. Glover)

PW8

On Sunday 9 August 1953, PW8 still stood on its low-loader looking as though a set of rails and some overhead cable would be all that was necessary to get it running again, even to Llandudno. Alas, it was never going to happen. Behind the works car are the neatly stacked upper and lower saloons of the trams that had been dismantled at Kyotts Lake Road Works over the preceding month. Careful examination reveals that the bogies and controllers had been removed from all the lower decks as these would be stripped, mainly for their valuable copper and brass. Soon afterwards the body remnants were burnt, but you, dear reader, have been saved any further distress by the omission of such a photograph. (A. N. H. Glover)

Endpiece

Although this book is devoted to the Coronation year of 1953, just to cheer everyone up, here is a selection of Birmingham tramcars in their pomp.

17
The Perry Barr terminus of the 6 route was outside the Crown & Cushion public house in Birchfield Road, just short of Perry Barr terminus. Known as 'The Aston Bogies', they were the first class of Birmingham Corporation tramcars. Built by ER&TCW as fifty-six-seat open toppers, they were transformed so that by the end of the 1920s they all had top-covers and were vestibuled. Car 17 was one of sixteen of these trams which were fitted with EMB Burnley bogies and fitted with 40 hp motors. This tram was one of only six of the 1-20 class to survive the Second World War and in 1947 stands at the Perry Barr terminus. (Burrows Brothers)

36
Car 36 was one of the original Brill tramcars of 1905 in its original condition as an open-topped, open balcony tram. It is working on the Cannon Hill service, which was opened on 1 January 1907. This was 'the great take over day' when some nine new Corporation electric tram routes were introduced, mostly taken over from the city of Birmingham Tramways Company. The tram is turning into Willows Road, opposite Cannon Hill Park. Partly hidden by the trees above the middle of the tramcar is a traction pole that was unique in Birmingham: it had two bracket arms at right angles to each other mounted on the same traction pole. (Commercial Postcard)

137 (Opposite, below)
On a rainy day in 1938, UEC-bodied tram 137 picks up passengers on the reserved track in the centre of Bordesley Green East. The route along Bordesley Green East was opened on 26 August 1928 and was the last extensive section of new track in Birmingham to be constructed, so it did seem rather strange that these 1907 tramcars were used on this most modern section on the system. The real reason for the continual use of four-wheelers on the 84 and 90 routes to Stechford was that the inner city parts of the routes were unsuited to bogie cars, especially the former route via Fazeley Street, which had restricted clearances on some of the sharp corners. As a result of this, these Stechford routes were usually operated by the older cars of the fleet, up until 1939 by those of the 71-220 class. Car 137, originally mounted on the unsuccessful Mountain & Gibson radial trucks retrucked with Peckham P35 units, has just dropped three passengers at the Kenwood Road stop on 1 April 1939 while working the 84 route. (A. N. H. Glover)

61

Standing outside the Railway Inn, at the terminus of the 32 Lodge Road route in Vittoria Street, in 1938 is car 61. The pub dated from 1900 and was all but surrounded by railway bridges and embankments in something of a backwater in Soho. Introduced in 1905 and were supplied by UEC as open-topped 48-seaters with DK6A 35 hp motors. They were mounted on 6-foot wheelbase Brill 21E trucks, but after a fatal accident in Warstone Lane in 1907 with car 22, fifty-four of the class were fitted with Maley track brakes. Although top-covered and vestibuled in the 1920s, their short wheelbases made them highly suitable for the tortuous curves on the Lodge road route. The problem of de-wiring on these corners was overcome when some of the class were fitted with bow-collectors. Seventeen of the class were retained after the rest of the 130 of the type were withdrawn and these trams, including car 61, survived until the closure of the Lodge Road route in March 1947. (D. R. Harvey Collection)

374
A typical four-wheel Birmingham tram was car 374. This tram entered service in January 1912; having been built by UEC as a low-height 40 hp car, it was mounted on 7 foot 6 inch UEC 'flexible-axle, swing-yoke' trucks. It is in Garrison Lane on 30 April 1939 when working on the 90 route to Stechford, having been transferred to Coventry Road depot from Witton only some three weeks earlier, having displaced the last of the 71-220 class trams on the Stechford services. The last forty of the 301-400 class were six inches longer to accommodate easier access to the hand brake on the platform. Some of this class survived until 1950, including car 374, which was withdrawn from service at Miller Street depot on 29 September 1950. (L. W. Perkins)

528 (Opposite, below)
Working on the 69 short working, along Bristol Road to and from Northfield, car 528 prepares to leave Northfield shopping centre on its way back to the city. Built in 1913 with an open balconied body by UEC, the tram was fitted with a GEC WT 32R 70 hp motor in 1927 for use on the West Bromwich and Wednesbury routes, where the tram schedules demanded a good turn of speed. When these routes closed in 1939, car 528 led a nomadic wartime existence, being allocated to the depots at Moseley Road, Rosebery Street and Witton before arriving at Selly Oak in November 1948 after having its body strengthened, resulting in the platform window being plated over. At Selly Oak this tram could show once again its real turn of speed on the Bristol Road reserved tracks, where speeds of up to 40 mph were regularly achieved. Along with the later air-brake trams, 528 and all the other 70 hp cars were withdrawn on 5 July 1952 when the Bristol Road group of services were abandoned. (G. F. Douglas)

407
Standing at the Alcester Lane's End terminus of the 42 route in front of the Kings Arms is car 407.
The driver and conductor, with his ticket rack, are both standing on the platform. Destination
boxes displaying route numbers were introduced in the middle of the Great War, while the name
BIRMINGHAM CORPORATION TRAMWAYS on the cream-painted rocker panel ceased to
be used in about 1920. These 40 hp UEC-bodied four-wheelers looked the same as the 301 class
trams but were mounted on Mountain & Gibson 7 foot 6 inch trucks. There were fifty in the
batch but they were modified in the latter half of 1913 with the fitting of the Spencer-Dawson
air and oil brake for use on the 1 in 13 gradient of Leopold Street. Car 407 would remain in
service until the closure of the Moseley Road routes on 1 October 1949. (Commercial Postcard)

752

Car 752 turns from Suffolk Street into Navigation Street towards the terminus shelters for the Bristol Road and Cotteridge services. This tram had a sixty-three-seat Brush totally-enclosed bodies with EMB Burnley bogies and DK30/1L 63 hp motors and entered service from Rosebery Street depot in early 1927. Although they looked much like previous totally-enclosed BCT bogie cars, the 732-761 class were the first in the fleet to be fitted with Maley air brakes. Having worked on the 33 route to Ladywood, 752 left Rosebery Street for Washwood Heath depot in December 1933 and was transferred to Selly Oak at the end of September 1942, where it remained until the closure of the Bristol Road routes on 5 July 1952. (D. R. Harvey Collection)

775 (Opposite)

Freshly repainted on 20 July 1943 is Brush-bodied air-brake car 775. It is standing at the terminus in Alum Rock Road at the Pelham public house. Although fresh out of the works, at least one window is boarded up as a result of a shortage of window glass. These EMB Burnley-type maximum traction bogie cars had air-brakes and 63 hp motors, but differed from the previous class by having eight windows in the upper saloon, rather than the more aesthetically pleasing four window layout. This was designed so that each row of seats in the upper saloon could have its own opening window to aid ventilation. These trams were a batch of fifty, numbered 762–811, that were delivered to Washwood Heath depot between September 1928 and February 1929 and were fitted with Fischer bow-collectors rather than trolleypoles for working on the Alum Rock and Washwood Heath services. (D. R. Harvey Collection)

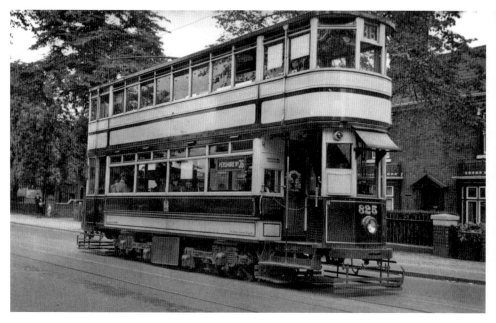

825

The final class of 'traditional' Birmingham bogie cars were numbered 812–841 and entered service between November 1928 and April 1929 and were the first trams ordered by Mr A. C. Baker, who unusually accepted a tender for the bodies from Short Brothers of Rochester. This seaplane manufacturer had never built tramcar bodies before, though they had supplied Birmingham Corporation with some 173 bus bodies mounted on either AEC 504 or 507 chassis. They had Maley & Taunton maximum traction bogies and that company's design for the air brake. The class had GEC DK30/1L 63 hp motors and, like the previous class, weighed 16 tons 15½ cwt. With its sun visor pulled down, car 825 is in Bristol Road working on the 36 service to Cotteridge on 7 August 1939. These thirty trams spent their entire lives based at Cotteridge depot and were withdrawn with all the other air brake cars when the Bristol Road and Cotteridge routes were abandoned on 5 July 1952. (E. C. Haywood)

843 (Opposite, below)

Parked at the Cotteridge terminus in 1944 is Birmingham's last numerical tramcar. Numbered 843, this was a Brush-bodied lightweight car which dated from 1930. It is standing almost underneath the blackout trough on the overhead although by this date, air raids on Birmingham had been over for nearly a year. The tram is fitted with a wartime headlight mask and has white painted fenders. Car 843 entered service in September 1930 and looked more like a smoothed profile version of one of the later standard Birmingham bogie tramcars. It weighed even less than its predecessor at 12 tons 6½ cwt, though this lightness of construction meant that it was always plagued by structural problems and it was taken out of service in January 1952, six months before the closure of the Cotteridge 36 route, because of a defective motor and signs of the body 'working'. (Burrows Brothers)

842

Looking in excellent condition, Birmingham's first lightweight tramcar, 842, turns into Kyotts Lake Road Works for the final time on 7 July 1952. 842 was the last tram to leave Cotteridge depot and run along Pershore Road. This magnificent tramcar had a Short Brothers sixty-three-seat body, DK T1905/3KP 40 hp motors and EE Burnley bogies. This 33 feet 6 inches long tramcar weighed 13 tons 12 cwt 1 qtr, which was just over three tons lighter than the standard Birmingham bogie cars. 842 entered service in November 1929 and was a contemporary of the 'Feltham' trams for LUT and Metropolitan and predated Liverpool's Cabin and Robinson bogie cars, Blackpool's 'Balloons', Glasgow's 'Coronation' trams and the Liverpool 'Green Goddesses' by around six years. In the depot is the tram, 395, which was already reserved for preservation. (G. F. Douglas)

Tailpiece

2489

4 July 2003 was the half-centenary of the abandonment of the Birmingham tram system. To commemorate this anniversary, the author took his preserved 1950 ex-Birmingham Crossley-bodied Crossley DD42/6, 2489 (JOJ 489), on a tour to each of the three former tram termini at Erdington, Pype Hayes and here at Short Heath. Crossleys from the same class had been used to begin the replacement buses from Steelhouse Lane and a similar bus, 2465 (JOJ 465), had been the first on the new 65 service, making it appropriate that 2489 was used on this re-enactment. 2489 stands at the present day terminus of the 65 route in Sheddington Road, just across Short Heath Road from the original tram terminus that was located in the distance behind the Crossley. It is hoped that the same trip around the last three Birmingham tram routes will take place on 4 July 2013 on the 60th anniversary of the tram car abandonment. (D. R. Harvey)